GET THE
HOME SOLD

Dedicated to my father James, my daughters Lilian & Amelia, and to the memory of my mother Judi.

First Edition Paperback June 2021

ISBN 978-1-7775047-3-1

Published by Domino Effect Publishing, All Rights Reserved

GET THE HOME

SOLD!

HOW TO SELL A HOUSE
USING TACTICS FROM
TOP REAL ESTATE AGENTS

Jeff Rout

Table of Contents

SECTION THREE:
LIST THE PROPERTY

SECTION FOUR:
MARKET THE PROPERTY

PREFACE

This book is intended to be used by both private home sellers and real estate agents with the objective of selling a property for the highest net revenue possible.

That might confuse some private sellers that are reading this book. Why write it for real estate agents as well? Don't real estate agents already know how to sell a house?

It's written for real estate agents as well as private sellers for two reasons. First, it is because private sellers and real estate agents ultimately have the same goal: to sell the property at the highest value possible. Second, it is because the tactics used to accomplish this goal can be used by both real estate agents and private sellers equally.

There is nothing magical that the top real estate agents do. It just takes know-how, dedication, experience, and hard work. This book focuses on the know-how part. You have to implement consistently what is in this book to get the rest.

As for the question "Don't real estate agents already know how to sell a house?" The answer is too often no.

Most real estate agents are not given any training on how to sell a property.

When they take their licensing exam, that exam is about law, rules, ethics, and industry practices. It doesn't discuss anything at all about how to actually sell a house.

Most real estate brokerages aren't any better in their training. When a real estate agent joins a brokerage, they are usually told to hit the streets and get clients. They aren't even told how to get clients, and they especially are not told how to sell the client's property. They are generally left on their own to figure that out.

Most training seminars that real estate agents take focus on how to get clients. Those seminars can be excellent for teaching that. But they don't usually take the next step and teach what works best to sell a house.

This is why there are still agents that only put up an MLS listing, advertise their listing in print or a website, and put up a lawn sign. Then they sit and wait for a deal to fall into their lap.

That style might sell the house. But not at the highest net revenue.

This book is to teach how to get those extra percentage points that make your sale get top return. It doesn't matter if you are selling your house yourself or if you are a real estate agent who wants to get your client the highest value possible by hiring you. (That's a good strategy, by the way, to get more and more clients. Really, if you want to know how to get clients, you should focus first on how to add the most value for your clients. Once you do that, more clients will follow.)

My intention was to write this book in a way that is applicable to both real estate agents and private sellers simultaneously. But some aspects are obviously more applicable to private sellers and vice versa. Rather than name my audience with each point in the book, I am just writing this here and will trust the reader will be able to determine by context who the audience is.

SECTION ONE

GET THE PROPERTY READY TO SELL

Chapter 1

TREAT YOUR HOME SALE LIKE A BUSINESS TRANSACTION

As soon as you decide to sell real estate it is vital to no longer think of the property as having any emotional or sentimental value. This is no longer about a cherished family home. This is now about selling a commodity.

Remove emotion from the equation.

For most people, their property has a certain level of sentimental value. After all, the property was your home. You invested your personality into the property. You had good times and bad times in it. You gathered with friends and family. Maybe you raised children in it. There are happy and sad memories attached to the home. These normal events can make the home feel extraordinary.

But when you are selling real estate you need to detach yourself from any sentimental feelings you may have for the property. Once you decide to sell, it's best to stop thinking of the property as a beloved home, but as a product that you are selling.

If you want to net the highest return you can get in real estate, you have to think of this now as strictly a business transaction.

The house you are selling is your product. home buyers are now your customers. The other houses on the market for sale are your competitors. Your Realtor is your sales team. And a significant part of your focus should be the bottom line.

Once we get into the mindset that this is a product, we can detach ourselves from many of the pitfalls involved in selling real estate.

Very often, you will get offers that are far less than your listed price. A home seller that is emotionally attached to the house or the transaction will feel insulted by that. We should never feel insulted by any offer. This is strictly business. If someone feels insulted they will not negotiate properly and might ruin what could have been worked into a workable deal. I've had offers that were 10% under the asking price where I was able to negotiate the deal to be within 1% of it. That ended up being right where the sellers wanted to sell. If they had scorned the offer because of feeling insulted, we never would have been able to make that deal happen.

Home buyers will critique every little thing about a house when they are in the process of purchasing. This can be sincere, but it can also just be a negotiating tactic that they will use to try to justify a lower purchase price. Either way, the best response is to treat this like a business transaction. You need to know the real value of your home to the market, and to act appropriately regarding selling the house to net the highest return. A home seller who is attached to the property emotionally will again be insulted, and that can again ruin what could turn into a workable deal.

A savvy home seller understands that the little quirks that they love about the property might not appeal to home buyers. Sometimes you need to put away something you love about the home to sell it best. Perhaps you have a massive collection of something. That collection might be wonderful, but to a home buyer, they will only see the property as cluttered. Perhaps you painted a mural on a wall that you love. It might not be what the new home buyer is going to want to look at every day. The individuality that you put into your home was great for when you are living in the home. But when you intend to sell the home, it might be time to put that individuality aside for your next home. We need to remove the emotion attached to that so that we can appeal to the home buyer, not to the home seller anymore.

Focus on the bottom line.

Which is better? To sell something for $100 and spend $20 doing it, netting $80? Or to sell something for $120 and spend $30 doing it, netting $90? Or to sell something for $130 and spend $60 doing it, netting $70?

Of course, the answer is to net $90. That's what you need to focus on: the bottom line.

This isn't being pedantic. Some expenses will not get your home sale an equal return for the costs. And some expenses will net you a higher return. So we want to focus on the expenses that have historically paid off, and avoid the expenses that don't.

That's pretty common sense.

But the fact is many homeowners get focused on the final gross sale price more than the net revenue. That's a mistake.

You do want to spend money where it is reasonably expected to net more money back to you than the cost. And you want to stay away from costs that don't give a positive return on investment.

The big question then becomes, what are the expenses that we usually see netting a positive return on investment? We will go over some of those items in the coming chapters. But the point here is to get into the proper mindset.

To net the highest return you can with your home sale, you need to remove emotion from the equation. Treat the sale strictly like a business transaction and focus on the bottom line.

Chapter 2

TIME TO DO SOME MAINTENANCE

Selling a house means it's time to be proactive about getting the house in good shape. Generally speaking, every house needs to have some work done to improve its appeal.

Most likely, the property we want to sell has some maintenance that it needs.

There's a saying in real estate that price fixes ugly. What it means is that for every defect a property has, it can usually be mitigated by a change in price – a downward change in price. And this is generally true.

But this book is about getting you the highest NET amount of money for your property. That's what really matters. So how do we do that in terms of repairs and renovations?

On one end, we can accept that price fixes ugly and put the property on the market in its current condition. Sometimes that can make sense. Maybe the property isn't in rough enough shape to warrant any repairs. Maybe the property is in such rough shape that renovations would cost more than can be spent by the seller, or more than would get a good return on their renovation investment. Those are perfectly reasonable positions.

On the other hand, we can spend and work to bring the property up to a show home condition to get the highest market price available. But even this isn't without flaws.

The highest market price doesn't always depend on the condition of the improvements on the land – the buildings in particular.

That seems like an odd statement, but it is true. The highest market price is determined by the best use of the land. And that might not be to have the type of house that is currently on the property. The best use of the land might be to tear down the current buildings and replace it with new improvements.

How do you know the best use of the land? The easiest and quickest method is to look around what else is there. If you're in a neighbourhood with mostly rentals, then a rental property is likely. If you're in a neighbourhood with luxury homes, that is likely what your buyer will want to. But you also want to know the zoning of the area and to know what, if any, development projects are happening in the area. They can easily affect the purchase and can lead to a massive return on your investment.

You don't always know the taste of your prospective buyer.

You might spend money upgrading the property and the buyer might not like those improvements. Some buyers just want to renovate the property themselves to make it theirs, but this is rare. Still, I have been involved in a few purchases with new upgrades that the buyers immediately removed and changed. So all that money spent on renovations was money wasted in those cases.

This means that expensive improvements might not bring any return at all. You need to know the market to know more about your most likely buyer.

So where does that leave us? Should we renovate or shouldn't we? Unfortunately, the answer is really that it all depends on your situation and who the likely buyer will be. But a very good rule of thumb is to do some renovations that meet a few criteria to mitigate the risks of overspending on renovations.

Decide on improvements with the best use of the land in mind.

We will go more into the best use of the land further ahead.

But, if the best use of the property is to tear down the buildings, there is no reason to do any improvements to those buildings. If the value of the property is land value only, then the quality of the building is irrelevant. Spending time and money to improve what is likely to be destroyed anyway isn't a good option.

Sometimes, we don't know if the best use is for a move-in ready buyer or a developer. In that case, leaning towards the cheap side of improvements can also make sense. If there's doubt, do the cheap, quick, and easy improvements, but you might not want to do much more than those.

Improve obvious defects.

I don't mean "can it be hidden?" We never, ever hide defects. I just mean is it something that is immediately and obviously visible? If you have an ugly splash of paint behind your furnace then that likely isn't that big a deal. It's in a place where it doesn't really matter to most buyers, so there's no point in investing time or money in something like that. But if the defect is obvious, then it's coming more into the realm of something that needs to be fixed.

Improve defects that are easily fixed.

So many issues with selling houses are small things that take no more than 5 minutes to fix: a creaky or sticky door, a light stain on the flooring, broken electrical coverings, etc. If they are cheap and easy fixes, then you should do them. An entire house can often have these renovations done in half a day and for less than a couple hundred dollars. That's time and money well spent and it is unlikely to be wasted.

Make improvements that you can do skillfully.

Can the seller make the renovations like a professional? If the seller can paint like a professional, then that could be the deciding factor on whether to paint or not. Maybe hiring a professional is too expensive in this case, but doing a professional job yourself isn't.

If you have a professional family member or friend that is willing to give you a discount then this can still apply.

However, if the seller can't do a professional job, then usually the answer is to either hire a professional or don't do it. An unprofessional job will likely not be doing any favours for the final sales price, and it might actually hurt it.

Fix defects that make the property appear unsound.

There's a difference between a chipped tile and defects that make the house itself seem broken. Leaky faucets and doors that don't close or open are a good example. When a home buyer sees those problems they often think to themselves that the property itself is broken. These defects should be fixed, even if you need to hire a professional to fix them.

Make renovations that will increase the value more than the cost of the renovations.

Are the renovations likely to increase the value of the house more than the cost of the renovations? In most cases, the answer is no. Most research suggests that for every $1000 a homeowner spends on renovations, they only improve the value of the property by $700 on average. If the homeowner has a professional skill, then that number can be reduced significantly, of course. This is why we have the rules above. Most renovations won't give a positive return on investment. But if the rules above apply, then they can.

Make the renovations based on your time horizon.

Do you have time for renovations? If you don't have the time or money to make renovations, and you have to sell quickly, then you likely don't have any choice but to sell the property without many renovations. In this type of case, I would almost always still recommend doing the quick, cheap, and easy repairs and renovations. Almost everyone has the time and money for that. But if not, that rather answers itself about whether to renovate or not.

To sum it up; should you do some renovations? If the defect is obvious, and the seller can easily fix it professionally, quickly, and cheaply; then yes, it should be renovated. If the defects will raise a doubt in the buyer's mind on the soundness of the property, those defects should be renovated. If the defects are a lack of soundness, then they must either be fixed or disclosed to the buyer.

If not, then you should seriously think about if it seems likely that those renovations will bring you any return on investment at all. The truth is that most renovations do not bring a dollar-for-dollar improvement in sales price compared to the cost of the renovation. So stick to the guidelines above, and you're likely to get a good net return on your time and money.

Chapter 3

Make the Property Bright and Spacious

If there is one piece of advice that always fits in terms of maximizing the appeal of a property, it is to make the property appear as bright and spacious as you reasonably can, while still following the guidelines of what to improve and what not to. A bright and spacious property is what buyers want to see most often, and the same style house where one property is made to look so will outsell a house that doesn't look so.

This isn't to say that you need to tear down the walls and change the layout. That type of renovation will likely not give you the same return for the cost unless you are a professional renovator. But you can do a few simple changes to help make the property show more bright and spacious.

To make the property appear bright and spacious without doing any major renovation changes; you only need to follow a few steps.

1. De-clutter the property.

2. If you are repainting, use neutral and light colours.

3. If you are repainting, finish the painting job a few weeks before your sale start date.

4. If you are re-doing floors, use neutral or bright colours.

5. Get the house as clean as possible.

If you do these steps, you will have a massive improvement on the showing quality of the property, and that means more and better offers.

Chapter 4

DECLUTTER THE PROPERTY

The first and best use of staging a property to sell it is simply to declutter the property. A home strewn with possessions will always seem more cramped and claustrophobic.

This is a simple step. It doesn't require much expense. No renovations are required. But this step will always improve how a property shows and is one of the most important steps available for a home seller.

As a real estate agent acting for a buyer, especially one interested in a rental property, I love a house that is cluttered. Because I know that this house will not show very well. It won't get as many offers, and the offers it does get will be much lower than the property itself deserves. So long as the property itself is in good condition, we should be able to buy such a property at a price lower than the market value. It's a great way to get more equity in the property you buy. You have to be able to look past the clutter, of course. For many buyers, they just can't do that.

So when acting for the seller, I always say to make sure the property isn't cluttered.

De-cluttering has benefits above just showing better.

It could have the added benefit of mentally preparing yourself for the fact that this property is soon not to be yours anymore. That could be another step in getting yourself in the mindset of treating this as a business.

It starts the packing process before you have to move, making the move itself smoother and easier.

So, where to start?

Get rid of what you don't really want or need anymore.

Most of the clutter in people's homes turns out to be things they haven't touched or used in years. If that's so, it probably shouldn't be there while you are working to sell the home.

Some people use this opportunity to get rid of these items from their lives entirely. Usually, these things aren't garbage. So you don't want to just toss them away.

But you might consider having a garage sale to help with the process of de-cluttering.

What doesn't sell, you might want to donate to a thrift store or charity.

That's a good, effective way to de-clutter your home from the get-go.

Remove your personal items.

Take your personal and family photos down from the walls. Leave the walls with more vacancy, or replace them with art. You don't want walls to be empty, usually. But you don't want them too crowded either. Usually, it is perfectly sufficient with just one or maybe two items.

Remove any personal collections. You might greatly enjoy your collections, and why not? But the person looking to buy the property probably doesn't have an interest in the same things that interest you. So your collection doesn't increase interest, but it does decrease the feeling of spaciousness. The collections have to be put away.

Take any eccentric or unusual decor down. The things that you have used to make the property yours have to be taken down. The person looking to buy it likely doesn't have the same taste. And the same reason these things help make the property yours will also make it feel like it isn't for the prospective buyer.

Remove unneeded or tattered furniture.

If you don't need the furniture, just have it removed. That will increase the space immediately. If the furniture looks bad, even though the furniture isn't usually part of the sale, it will reduce the overall appeal of the property and is best removed as well.

Set up rooms for their correct purpose.

You might be using a bedroom as an office. But it will appeal more to most home buyers if it is set up for its property purpose.

That being said, you might need to have your rooms set up as they are for your ability to work. That's legitimate. But understand that keeping it so is a point that will reduce the selling appeal to most buyers.

For the bedrooms:

Clean out your closets.

A very big sales feature is a closet that looks spacious. Always. And the easiest way to make a closet look spacious is to have it no more than half full. So firstly, take out anything that doesn't belong in a closet.

Then take out clothes you don't wear often until the closet is only about half full. Now, regardless of the closet size, it looks more spacious to the viewer than it did when it was packed.

Don't have anything showing from under the bed.

It isn't a big deal if you store things under the bed. Most buyers do not ever take a peek under the beds. But you don't want anything that you are storing under the bed to be visible at all. You want them well hidden away.

Remove any toys.

As best as you can, don't have any toys visible. If you can't avoid that, have them neat and organized.

For the bathroom:

Throw out any unneeded toiletries.

If you have any expired or generally no longer wanted toiletries, now is the time to dispose of them.

Have nothing on the bathroom sinks except one soap dispenser.

Keeping a clean and uncluttered bathroom has a huge effect on how well the house shows. Generally speaking, bathrooms and kitchens are big selling features in a home, so having it show its best is important.

Remove all toothbrushes, toothpaste, make-up, etc from the bathroom countertop. We want it empty and clean.

Put all that stuff out of view. You can put it in a cupboard under the sink, as that isn't something that will go through the same scrutiny. But even that you don't want to be cramped.

Arrange clean towels neatly.

Only have a minimal amount of towels out. Keep them fresh and clean, and have them placed neatly and orderly on the hanger. Use small and thin towels to not have them bulge out.

For the garage:

Remove everything in the garage that can be removed.

Very often, we use garages as storage spaces. But that won't help us sell the property. We need to move everything we've stored in the garage out.

If you've built a workstation in the garage, that can stay. But clean it up and remove all the clutter from that station as well.

What isn't removed should be stored cleanly and neatly.

Store whatever remains in a suitable storage container. Make sure they don't take up much space and keep them as out of the way as you possibly can.

Your potential buyers want to make sure their cars and stuff can fit in the garage. If you have all your stuff in there, they won't be able to imagine where theirs can fit.

For the kitchen:

Clear off the kitchen countertops.

Get rid of the items on your counter that might be convenient to you while cooking, but take away any counter space. There shouldn't be anything on the counter at all. Remove all appliances and put them into a closed cabinet.

We want the prospective buyers to be able to see the entirety of the countertop. That makes them think it is the biggest, and that helps them imagine their own gear being able to fit with room to spare in your property.

Clear up the fridge.

Artwork, calendars, magnets and all should be removed from the fridge. You can get away with one or two things if they are vital to your day-to-day use of the kitchen. But if they aren't, take them down.

Keep the inside of the fridge clean, orderly, and uncluttered as well. People will be opening your fridge to see the interior of it.

Organize the kitchen cabinets.

Anything that isn't used frequently in the cabinets should be removed. Everything else that is staying should be organized. You could probably get away with not having as many things in the cabinets. So taking out half of the plates, bowls, and cups and putting them into storage will instantly make your cupboard seem more spacious and ready to meet the needs of your buyers.

For the hallway:

Put away unused shoes.

Any shoes you haven't used recently should be removed. You generally don't need all your shoes out at the same time. Only have out what you need, and put those away neatly too.

Clear out any mail, key, or clothing piles.

Any post has to be removed from the entryway. As well as piles of keys or clothing. Put all these things out of sight.

Clean up and clear out the closets.

Pack up anything you aren't using frequently. Remove anything that doesn't belong in the hallway closets. Try to get the closet to only be half full.

For the yards:

Get rid of as much as you reasonably can.

An empty deck will sell better than a deck cluttered with furniture. So remove anything that you readily can. Keep only what you use regularly.

Clean and organize the shed.

Pack up as much as you can. Most of the things in the shed are seasonal and you aren't using them right now, so remove them so the shed seems bigger.

And finally:

Whatever isn't being removed has to be organized.

Make sure there is reasonable space for everything and have everything in its place. Items that are well-organized look less cluttered and make the space seem bigger.

What to do with the stuff you've decluttered?

For the things you do want or need, the best solution is to store them off-site: a storage facility, with a moving company, or at the new moving location if possible.

If you can't do those things, then the best bet is to keep them stored on-site but as out of the way as you possibly can. You don't want piles of boxes forming a new cluttering.

Chapter 5

GIVE THE PROPERTY A GOOD CLEANING

Cleanliness is next to Godliness, so they say. And cleanliness is certainly one of the top priorities in selling a home.

Now that all the clutter has been removed and the home is organized, it's time to clean it up. The home does need to be very clean to show best.

Buyers are often less willing to look past a dirty, cluttered home than they are most other things. It is also something that is not very expensive to do. So keeping the house clean is an absolute must if you want to get top market value.

Keep the property clean throughout showings.

Cleaning isn't a one-time thing. The property should be kept clean throughout the sales process. That means doing the little touch-ups each and every day for whatever mess was made. It also means doing a weekly 'big clean' to keep the property in a show state.

I go even further in saying that you should keep the property clean at all times. Don't leave the door with a dirty house. You may get a call from a buyer to see the property right away and you won't have time to clean it. So keep it clean at all times so that if you get a request for a showing with little notice, you can still show the property to that customer.

If you get a request for a showing, even if the property is a little dirty and cluttered, it is probably best to try to accommodate the request. Being the first to show is usually a good thing. That customer is likely going to see other properties as well and you might not get a second chance.

A dirty house means you likely won't get as good an offer. But a not as good offer is better than no offer. So, within reason, I recommend showing the house even if you have let it get a little dirty.

The best option is to keep it spic and span clean and ready to show. The second best option is to show it even if it has a little mess here and there.

Wash the windows.

Sellers often forget to get their windows clean, but it's a very important step.

Buyers will be looking out those windows into the backyard. If the windows are smudged and dirty, their impression of your property will be less than it otherwise would have been with clean windows.

Hire a professional cleaner if you are unable to clean the property properly yourself.

People have busy lives and they can't always devote the time needed to get the property clean for whatever reason. When this is the case, it is best to hire a professional to come and clean the property.

When we look at return on investment, hiring a professional cleaner – which costs a few hundred dollars – compared to not having a clean property, has a very high return on investment.

You shouldn't always do renovations, but you should always clean the property; if necessary using a professional cleaning service.

Chapter 6

MAKE THE PROPERTY ODOUR-FREE

A pungent aroma will hit your customers walking into the property and it can often be the first thing they will mention. It is very difficult to change a first impression, so odours have to be managed when selling your house.

Bad smells give a very bad impression.

Once people smell a bad odour, they will immediately think that there are deep-rooted problems in the house. Odours aren't associated with just what is in the house, people associate them with the house itself. So if a house smells bad, people will think it *is* bad.

People also believe that smells can't be changed. That isn't the truth, of course. You can eliminate odours in a house. But when people are viewing a house they tend to get into the mindset that this is a permanent element of the property. That will turn off most buyers, and will certainly undercut any offers.

You need to get rid of the root cause of odours, and not rely on sprays or de-odourants.

You can't mask up the odour and expect the property to sell at top price.

People often think that if they can smell these de-odourants, that there must be a problem that you are covering up. So even if you don't have a bad smell in the house, they will think you do with the presence of these.

Band-aid solutions to smells like sprays and such are better than just having bad smells. But they aren't a good solution and they certainly won't net you the top value that you otherwise could get.

No, you need to get rid of the causes of the smell. That's the best method, and that's what this chapter is about.

Stop smoking in the house.

The first and most obvious advice is to stop smoking in the house. This is a major cause of odours and is difficult to remove. Smoke tends to stick to the walls, ceiling, and floors themselves.

If you want to sell your property for top dollar, it needs to be a smoke-free property.

If you must smoke, smoke outside and well away from the house so no smoke gets inside. It doesn't matter if the doors are closed, the smoke will get inside.

Don't smoke in the garage thinking that's an ok place to do so. Firstly, smoke will again get inside the house. Additionally, as soon as the buyers open the garage door they will be hit with that smell. When I've shown houses where the occupant smoked in the garage, the buyers often didn't even want to go inside the garage. They wrote those houses off and weren't interested in buying them.

So no smoking in the house.

Clean up dirty laundry.

Of course, this goes along with the removing clutter step. But these steps all work very well together in helping you get the best dollar for your house.

Dirty laundry lying around will cause a smell – especially with families that exercise or are involved with water and get wet clothing and towels. Get the clothes into the washer sooner than later.

Do the dishes right away.

Again, this fits with not having clutter. Get the dishes done right away and keep those smells from spoiling your potential home sale.

Clean the fabric on your upholstery.

Get all your furniture cleaned. Most often, a simple cleaning with a vacuum and a fabric spray is sufficient. But you need to evaluate the situation and see if you need more.

If you do need more due to seriously bad smells, you need to hire a professional cleaner to clean up that furniture. Or you can get rid of it if it smells – either by storing it off the property, selling it, donating it, or disposing of it.

Wash all your bedsheets.

Run all your linen and sheets through the washer. Also, wash all your duvets and quilts – bring them to a dry cleaner if you need to.

Keep your fridge odour-free.

Make sure there is no expired food or drink in the fridge. Get rid of any particularly pungent food. Fish and spicy foods are common causes. They may smell delicious to you and everyone who shares your appetite but your customer very well might not, and those might make them feel nauseated.

You don't want to spoil a sale to pungent food smells. Remove them from the fridge.

Now that you've removed the causes of odours, it's time to get rid of the lingering odours.

The bad smells will persist even after you've removed their cause. That's why buyers often think that bad smells can't be remedied. So even after you've removed the causes, you still need to get rid of those lingering odours.

Clean or remove the carpets.

Carpets are a major battery of odours. They tend to keep whatever was spilled on them, rubbed on them, or even what was in the air around them. You need to clean them, or if necessary remove them.

If they aren't too bad, a simple steam cleaning will do. You don't need to hire a professional if they aren't that bad.

But if they are, then you have to grade them. If they are so bad that even a professional cleaning won't fix them, then you have to remove them and replace them with another flooring. It can be carpet again if you choose, but it must be replaced.

Replacing a stained and smelly carpet is usually a renovation that can bring a positive net return. But even there you have to use some judgement. If there are just one or two stain spots, the cost of the renovation might not bring you a positive return. But if there are many of them, it will usually pay off to get them replaced.

Get rid of smells in the walls.

If the walls have smells they need to be cleaned. You will have to scrub the walls with an agent that won't damage the wall surface but will help reduce or eliminate odours.

If you're hiring a professional to clean the house, you may want to include this task in their service as well.

Repaint the walls and ceiling if needed.

The smells can be reduced or eliminated by a fresh coat of paint. You don't usually need to go to this level just for smells on the walls. But for ceilings, this is usually the quickest and easiest way.

If you don't have smoke, pets, or pungent food smells in the house, then you usually don't have to worry about too much odour being in the ceiling, though.

Open up the doors and windows to completely flush out the air.

One of the easiest ways to get rid of smells is to completely re-cycle all the air that is in the house with fresh air from outside. Of course, the air outside has to smell better than what is inside for this to work. But just open the windows and doors for enough time to freshen up the air.

Put down some 'odour-traps' around the house, especially the trouble areas.

If just refreshing the air isn't enough, this is a pretty low-cost solution that can help.

Bowls of baking soda are very well known for their ability to absorb odours from the air. Vinegar can do the same, but it leaves its own vinegar smell.

This can be as simple as buying some boxes of baking soda and leaving them open in different places in the house. Concentrate them in the problem spots, but it doesn't hurt to have them scattered throughout the house as well.

If you do this, make sure you remove them before you start showing the house.

Get an ozone treatment for the house.

For the top of the line solution, ozone treatment can be very effective at reducing odours. Ozone doesn't mask odours, it destroys them. It is a go-to treatment for situations with serious odour issues – including smoke damage from a fire. The oxidation process breaks down the molecular structure of bacteria, viruses, and bad odours, thereby neutralizing them. An ozone generator can remove odours from cigarettes, pets, decay, and even skunks. It is generally effective against most any odour you're likely to encounter in a house – provided the source of the smell is also already removed. An ozone generator is used to create the ozone, which permeates the air and any surfaces in the area. The odour is neutralized and any bacteria and viruses are usually killed.

This treatment is much more expensive than the other issues described, so it isn't for everyone. But it is highly effective.

Ozone can be dangerous to breathe, and using ozone to remove odours takes a larger dosage than simply using it to sanitize the air you want to breathe. As such, ozone treatment for removing odours should only be used by someone who is experienced in the process.

It shouldn't be used in occupied areas. That means the property should not be occupied while this treatment is being done. It will not be safe for people, animals, or even plants to be on the premises during this treatment. That usually isn't a problem, for most circumstances, the generator can just be on when the occupants are at work. Multi-day treatments are not needed except in the worst cases.

Properties with shared ventilation must have that ventilation mitigated before any ozone treatment. Again, let a professional who is experienced in this manage this treatment if you must do it. It shouldn't be done by yourself unless you do this as your profession.

Don't use sprays or perfumes in the house to mask a scent if you can avoid it.

A spray or perfume in the air is better than nothing when dealing with bad smells. But it isn't a good option. As stated previously, most buyers will get a little suspicious with those and wonder what it is trying to cover up.

Additionally, some buyers will be allergic to those scents as well, and will react when seeing the home. Very often, they will want to leave quickly rather than seeing the house at all. While this isn't the majority of buyers, it is a significant enough percentage of them to warrant not using this method. After all, the buyer that just left because of the perfume may have been the one who wanted to buy your house if they had been able to see it.

Getting rid of odours is usually a cost that will pay off.

While I stated earlier that most renovation costs don't pay even pay for themselves, let alone create a profit. That isn't the case when dealing with odours.

A bad smell in a property is a quick turn-off for most buyers, and it is one of the hardest for them to see past. Offers on houses with smells will not be at the same level as offers on the exact same house if it didn't have a smell.

All in all, if you want to get the top market value for your property, you should seriously consider bringing your property to an odour-free state.

There are many options available to a home seller, and which option is best is determined by the needs of the house, and the budget of the seller. But one thing is certain, a house with odours will not sell at the top market price available.

Chapter 7

CLEAN OR REPLACE THE FLOORING

Now we have to work on the flooring. Buyers look at flooring as an indicator of the well-being of the house. If the house has bad flooring, it feels like it isn't well taken care of.

But the questions asked are: Should you replace the flooring? Should you clean the flooring? Should you just sell it as it is?

Unless your flooring is perfect and immaculate, you shouldn't sell it just as it is. It likely needs some touch-up.

So that brings us down to just cleaning the flooring or replacing it. Which will net you a better return on your house?

If the flooring is in reasonably good shape and is marketable, then a good cleaning is the best bet.

But what is reasonably good shape? And what is marketable?

Replace the flooring if it is ugly, smelly, dated, or seriously stained.

This is one of the cases where you will likely see a good return on investment for your renovations. Any flooring that is ugly, dated, or seriously stained can get you a positive return on the costs of updating the flooring.

If you can clean out those issues instead of replacing them, then that is the better solution. But if a cleaning doesn't correct them, they have to be replaced to get the top market price in the sale.

If you replace carpeting, it should be a neutral colour.

Light, neutral colours help with the objective of making the home feel bright and spacious. But you should avoid a carpet that is white, or even too close to white. It looks out of place usually, and will clash with anything other than black, grey, or white furniture. Also, buyers are worried about it the difficulty in maintaining it.

A light beige is best. But taupe or a warm grey tone can also work.

If this describes your carpet, you can stick with a cleaning unless it has serious stains.

If you are replacing the flooring, go with what will get you the best return on your dollar in the sale.

If you are going through the work of tearing out one flooring and putting in another anyway, you might also consider upgrading to flooring that will help sell the home.

Generally speaking, hardwood flooring and laminate flooring impress buyers the most.

Hardwood impresses the most, but there isn't much difference in many situations on how buyers see laminate flooring compared to hardwood. And there is a significant difference in cost.

So for many houses, a really good choice is laminate flooring. But you need to match the flooring to the house. An executive-level house will be almost expected to have hardwood. And the higher the quality of the house the higher that expectation will be.

However, modern laminate is even making that distinction matter less and less as the quality divide decreases. Meaning, in terms of return on investment, laminate flooring often does fairly well.

If you are putting in carpet, you don't need to buy top of the line.

A real estate resale secret: even cheaper carpet looks great when it's brand new. So if you are going to choose carpet, you don't need to pick the most expensive options out there.

You do want to have decent flooring. If you already have that, you're fine. If you don't, you should think about cleaning it as the first option because it is quicker, easier, and cheaper. But if a cleaning won't bring the carpet up to quality, you should consider replacing it and perhaps improving it.

Chapter 8

Install 100w Lights Everywhere

Remember the goal of showing the property at its best is for it to show bright and spacious. Probably the cheapest and easiest way to do that is to install bright lights throughout the house. Any light fixtures that have less than 100W lightbulbs should be replaced with 100W.

Pick either incandescent or LED lightbulbs. Generally, stay away from fluorescent. In my experience, they tend not to show the property well. You aren't installing these lights as a long-term solution in saving energy, so if you save money using incandescents, that's just fine for this purpose.

Don't install 100W lights anywhere that wouldn't be safe, of course.

Chapter 9

Repainting the Interior

We want the property to show at its best. Walls that need repainting do not give a good impression. Peeling paint, scratches, stains, etc, will give the impression that just as the walls needed more care than they got, the whole house needs more care than it got. It makes buyers think the house is not well maintained, and they might be buying a money pit.

Painting the interior walls can have a tremendous benefit to the resale value of your home, and it can be cost-effective as well.

If your walls look reasonably good, then you can skip this step. As always, you need to judge if the walls need enough work to justify the cost.

If you decide to repaint, here are a few simple rules to remember.

Most buyers do not want to have a paint job for the house they are buying.

The majority of home buyers are looking for move-in ready homes. They are not looking for more work. And the only ones that are willing to accept a house that comes with a great deal of work are those that also want a great deal in the price.

So don't hesitate to paint the walls thinking you will turn off the buyers. You won't. They want the house ready to move into.

Make sure it's a professional job.

That doesn't mean that you have to hire a professional painter. This is a job that can work with a Do-It-Yourself attitude. But there is a saying: 'The only thing more expensive than hiring a professional is not hiring one.' It's a good saying. It acknowledges that hiring a professional has a cost. But often that is even less of a cost than not hiring one.

So you can do this job yourself, but you must be able to provide a professional level job. It needs to look perfect. If you know that you can do that level of painting job, and you know that because you've done it many times before, then doing it yourself is fine.

But if you don't know that and you haven't done it many times before, you should hire a professional. An unprofessional paint job will be worse than not repainting. An unprofessional job will again make people think you are covering something up, and they will hesitate to give a good offer.

If you are going to repaint, it has to be of professional quality or nothing.

Focus on the kitchen, bathrooms, and high traffic areas on the property.

The areas that see the most traffic are the areas that buyers will also see the most. So if you only have limited time, those are where to focus.

Also, good-looking bathrooms and good-looking kitchens help sell a house more than the other rooms.

Do not use painting as a means of concealing material defects.

Never use paint as a means to conceal a defect with the property. You have an obligation to tell any buyer about any defects in the property.

But that doesn't mean you can't use paint to touch up after a defect has been corrected.

I had a client who had some water damage from a leaky pipe in their main floor ceiling. The first order of business was to correct the defect – to fix the leaky pipe. They had this done professionally, which is what I would only recommend in terms of correcting defects. Once the pipe was corrected, and there was no longer a leak, they replaced the ceiling material and painted it over. It looked brand new. That is an acceptable means of using paint.

Painting over the ceiling where the water damage was showing without correcting the issue is never acceptable. Painting over an area that has been corrected is acceptable.

Finish repainting at least a week before the house is going on the market.

Buyers do want to see a good paint job. But they don't want to see fresh paint.

Fresh paint always brings into their minds that the seller is hiding something. Of course, that isn't usually the case at all. Usually, it's just to improve the look of the house while they sell it, which is perfectly understandable.

But the fact that buyers will think this way can't be avoided. So avoid the trouble and give enough time for the paint to dry completely before you take pictures and put it on the market.

Also, make sure the paint job is done before you take the pictures to advertise the property. You want the pictures to be the best looking they can be. You want them to be an accurate representation of the property. And you don't want to give an obvious clue that the walls were just recently painted for the same reason as above.

Choose mostly light and neutral colours.

Remember our goal is to make the house look bright and spacious. So light and neutral colours work best. Additionally, light and neutral colours appeal to the largest percentage of home buyers, and that's exactly what we want to do.

That isn't to say you can't have a splash of colour with an accent wall. That can work, and I have rarely heard significant complaints from any buyers when we encounter them. Even when buyers have expressed they didn't like the colour of the accent wall, it hasn't acted as an impediment to their decision to buy the house. This suggests that when the colour of accent walls doesn't agree with the prospective buyer, it seems like a minor issue that they can look past. But an entire house that has a bad paint job will seem like a very large issue.

Unless your house already has a reasonably good paint job, you will likely benefit from a good return in selling the house if you paint the walls first. Make it professional, and make it appeal to the largest audience possible for the best success.

Chapter 10

Improve Your Curb Appeal

This is the essence of the idea that you can never make a second first impression. Building up your curb appeal is a great way to improve the offers your house will receive and it is often not that expensive to do.

Curb appeal is the immediate attractiveness of the property when looked at as a whole. It's also one of the most important aspects of getting the best sales price.

A good curb appeal sparks interest in the house and people become excited to see what is inside. A bad curb appeal often means buyers will tell their agent to just move on to the next one – no need to see inside this house.

So we need to make that first impression a good one to maximize our sale.

Keep in mind the costs of improving the curb appeal.

As always, cost has to be a consideration here. We want to do what is best to improve the curb appeal while also making sure we get a positive return on what we spend. If an improvement to the house will not give a positive return on that cost, then that improvement shouldn't be made.

Cleanliness and orderliness are vital.

Just like with the interior, the exterior needs to show clean and tidy, and for all the same reasons. Luckily, again, this is also a pretty cheap and easy step to take care of.

Wash the exterior of the house.

Most houses aren't washed regularly, and they often turn just a little darker because of that. It usually so even that people don't even know just how much dirt is often on their house.

Get a power washer and spray down the house from top to bottom. Very often, this act alone will make the house look brand new.

Remove all clutter from the yard.

Let's make that yard show spacious as well. Get rid of any toys or ornaments that take up space in the yard. You can keep a few ornaments out if you insist, but simplify, simplify is the name of the game here.

Try to find a balance between having too much yard furniture and too little. Too much will make the yard appear cluttered, crowded, and small. But too little furniture can make it feel uninviting, and perhaps even neglected. You want the yard to feel spacious and you don't want people to have to walk around things.

Consider repairing the roof.

If the roof looks rough, and shingles are missing or peeling, then you might want to consider repairing the roof. Again, this is a matter of benefit to cost. If this is a small issue, you might not get a positive return for the cost.

However, if the roof is leaking, you want to get that repaired. You are going to have to disclose that to your buyer anyway, and they won't want that. Generally speaking, buyers want a move-in ready property. Roofs that need fixing don't fit that.

Take care of the vegetation and plants.

Get the vegetation, bushes, and trees trimmed and looking well maintained. This is usually a very quick, easy, and cheap fix. Generally, this is one a person can do themselves without much risk.

Rake up all the leaves. Weed the lawn and the garden. Mow the lawn. Again, no need to spend much money, they can be done by yourself.

Trim the branches of any trees that are touching the house, and perhaps any that hang over the house as well.

Plant some bright and fragrant flowers.

Planting some new flowers and greenery will add colour and brightness to the house at very little cost, and will appeal to most buyers.

Fresh smelling flowers will also add a homey appeal to most buyers.

You want the buyer's experience to be pleasant right from the beginning. Flowers help make that happen.

You don't need to spend money on landscaping at this point.

Generally speaking, landscaping at this point is going to cost you more than you will benefit when selling the house. So this is a step you can skip in most circumstances.

Paint the front door and the garage door.

If the front and garage doors are looking rough, havingthem pop with a fresh coat of paint is probably one of the easiest and cheapest improvements you can make in improving the curb appeal of the property.

Likewise, a garage door with good paint makes the whole house look better.

If the doors already look great, you can skip this. If you do paint, always make sure it is a professional-quality job.

Paint the rest of the exterior if needed.

If cleaning the exterior won't give it enough of a new look, you might want to consider painting the exterior.

Just like the interior, you might do well with a fresh coat of paint on the outside of the house. Fresh paint will make the house look brand new. Give it time to dry, just like before, and also make sure it is done with professional-quality. If it isn't professional quality, you're better off not doing it at all in most cases.

You have many more options for colour on the outside than you do for the inside. You can also have a scheme of different colours on different aspects of the house. Always keep in mind that you want to appeal to as many buyers as possible, so stay away from colours that are just too outside the norm in your area. But a well-painted house has curb appeal with more give in the colour choice.

Also like the exterior, when painting, paint it before you take photographs and give it time to dry before you list it.

Repair and paint the fences.

Make sure the fences are upright and strong. Give them a fresh coat of paint to make them look new again. On this front, you can get away with a less professional-looking paint job in most circumstances. So even if you aren't a pro painter, but can still do a reasonable job, you can have at this one yourself.

Examine the door handles and doorbells.

You want the entrance to look great. And it isn't that expensive to make it look great.

In addition to painting, look at the door furniture. Does it look new and vibrant? Or does it look weathered? Touching up or even replacing the furniture is not that expensive, but it does add to the first impression you will get with the property.

Make sure the doorbell looks new and well cared for. Also, make sure it works. Buyers will be testing it. If it doesn't work, it gives the impression that there are problems with the house.

Roll out the welcome mat!

Having a clean and new-looking welcome mat is an easy touch to improve the first impression for any buyer. It's also very cheap and easy to do.

The tremendous benefit of making a good impression when selling a property cannot be overstated. No seller wants potential buyers to choose to not even see inside the house because it lacked adequate curb appeal. But some sellers don't focus on this aspect and so they lose a competitive edge.

Grab that advantage over your competition and make sure your house has the curb appeal that instantly grabs a buyer's attention and makes them want to see more.

SECTION TWO

KNOW THE MARKET

Chapter 11

KEEP UPDATED ON INVENTORY

A good means to know how to best market your property is to have strong knowledge of what else is being sold in your area. Remember from the previous section that once you start selling real estate, you have to think of all other home sellers as your competitors. So you need to know what the competition looks like. This is the very first step in your market research.

You need to know all of the following factors. What is the total number of properties currently on the market? What is the average number of properties for sale on the market in the area historically? What is the number of new listings that came on the market in the last 30 and 90 days and the number of properties that sold in the last 30 and 90 days? What is the average days on market for a property to sell in the area? What is the percentage of properties that have expired/cancelled/withdrawn for both the last 90 days and the last 12 months?

Each of those factors will be needed to have the most effective marketing plan. We will go over what each of those tells us.

How many properties are currently on the market?

This tells us how saturated the market is; how much competition will we have. If the inventory is lower than is the norm historically, then you may have a seller's market. If the inventory is higher than is the norm historically, then you may have a buyers market.

This alone doesn't tell you if it is a buyer's or seller's market because sometimes many people start selling their homes during a real estate boom to cash in on it. You do need more information than just this, but this is still a vital piece of information.

How many new properties have come onto the market in the last 30 and 90 days? How many have sold?

This is also a vital piece of information. If more houses are coming onto the market than are selling, then the inventory of housing is increasing. This could be (but again, isn't always) a sign of a market that could be moving more towards a buyer's market. If more houses have been sold than have come onto the market, then this could be a sign of a market moving more towards a seller's market.

What is the average number of days on the market for the properties that sold? How does this compare to the average for the broader area?

The average days on market for a home to sell will vary for every area. There are some areas where it will be within a month or two, and there are some where it is many, many months on average.

We want to know both of these answers for a few reasons. The average number of days recently gives us an idea of what we can expect in terms of getting an offer if you market the house properly. The average number of days currently compared to historically gives us a hint of whether we are operating in a buyer's market or a seller's market.

What is the number of properties that have failed to sell?

The expired house list tells us also a vital piece of information in the marketing plan. How many home sellers attempted to sell, but failed? If that number is high, then we might be looking at a buyer's market.

Researching the expired houses is also important because it can also tell us clues as to what price is a price that won't sell in the current market. We want to research those expired listings to find out why they didn't sell. Usually, it comes down to just two things: price and marketing. If the price is too high for that specific property, then the marketing doesn't matter; it won't sell. If the price is not too high, and other houses sold in the area, then it was likely a lack of thorough marketing that made the difference.

Keep a daily eye on each change on these parameters in the market.

You want to have a daily update on new properties on the market, sold properties, expired/cancelled/withdrawn listings. In real estate, these are called the *hot sheets*.

You need to keep up to date, and the market changes daily. The only way to keep your pulse on the real estate market is to read the hot sheets each day and see if it is going to affect your marketing plan. If it is, adjust accordingly.

Chapter 12

PREVIEW PROPERTIES

While it is essential to know the stats of the real estate market in your area, it isn't all you need to know. The stats show a general and average trend in the area, but the property you're selling is unique. Even if it has the exact same layout as every other property in the area, it would still be unique simply by virtue of its location. There are no two properties that are exactly the same.

So selling real estate isn't like selling gold. No one cares about getting this gold bar or that gold bar. They are only interested in the quality and weight of it.

Not so with real estate. Each property is unique, so you can't rely only on the stats to be able to properly and effectively come up with a price or marketing plan for the property unless you have personally seen the other houses on the market now, and for the last year or so in the past as well.

What this means is, **if you don't preview properties, you don't really deal in real estate.**

So you need to preview properties on at least a monthly basis to get an actual understanding of the market in the area. This is an area where real estate agents gain a significant portion of their market knowledge. Just by the nature of their business, they have to go in and out of properties on the market constantly; often even daily.

But for the person looking to sell their own home, they don't have that same ability to know the market. It just isn't possible. So what's the next best thing?

Since home sellers cannot be reasonably expected to have been previewing properties monthly to get a good knowledge of the properties in the area, they have to rely on previewing the properties that are available currently.

The best way to do that is to attend open houses.

Open houses are an invitation for you to preview the home. They don't require that you have any interest in buying the property. They don't inconvenience the home seller. It's an honest way to preview the properties in your area.

I don't like the idea of arranging viewings with other homes for sale outside of an open house. Some people recommend doing this, but I do not.

Firstly, it doesn't seem honest to me. The home seller is expecting to show houses to people who are interested in buying. They aren't expecting to show houses to people just so they can gain some market insight. I suppose a workaround for this issue is just to be honest and upfront that you aren't interested in buying and are only viewing the property to see what the competition is. But I wouldn't expect any home seller to set up a viewing in that case.

Setting up viewings takes a good deal of effort on the part of the home seller. We shouldn't expect that they are willing to put forth that effort just so we have a better understanding of market conditions. And we should also ask ourselves if we would want people to be calling us to arrange viewings and to inconvenience us, just so they can preview the property with no interest in ever buying it. I would say we likely wouldn't. So we should treat others as we want to be treated and not use this tactic. We can stick to open houses; those are fair game.

Chapter 13

Know the Real Value of the Property

Now that you have all the market research you need, you should be able to come to the real value of the property.

One common error that some home sellers make is to simply take the average price per square foot and apply that figure to their home and slap that price on it. While the price per square foot is a factor, that isn't how to calculate the true value of the property.

I don't think that a non-professional has the tools to properly evaluate the value of their real estate. I had to take a rather exhaustive course on home pricing before I had the know-how. Real estate appraisers here in Alberta must pass a thorough licensing program before they are permitted to act as an appraiser. It isn't as simple as finding averages in prices. And the techniques used would require an entire book of their own, not a chapter.

Some for sale by owners prefer to do this entirely on their own, and that is usually not a wise decision. Remember, we treat the sale of real estate like a business transaction. Smart businessmen always get professional consultation. This is a topic that requires professional input.

There are only a few real options in terms of getting a professional analysis on the market value of the property.

One option is to hire a real estate agent.

If you hire a real estate agent, then you aren't really a for-sale-by-owner anymore. But that will get the job done.

The benefit of hiring a real estate agent is that they often only charge for the successful sale of your home, meaning there is no upfront cost. They take the risk that they won't be paid for their work, not you. If you hire an appraiser, that will have an upfront cost.

Another option is get free CMAs from real estate agents.

You could interview different real estate agents and ask them for a CMA – a Comparative Market Analysis. This isn't an appraisal, but it is the tool that real estate agents will use in evaluating the property they want to sell.

If you go this route, there's nothing wrong with it, but I think the only ethical way to do this is to be upfront that you are considering selling the house yourself. It isn't fair to ask anyone to do work for you for nothing. You wouldn't want that in your job, so treat others as you want to be treated. But if you are upfront on this, it seems perfectly fair to me.

A third option is to hire an appraiser.

If you want to remain a for-sale-by-owner, then hiring a real estate appraiser is the best bet. One added bonus of using a real estate appraiser is you can share the appraisal (if allowed in the deal with the appraiser) with prospective buyers. This can give them peace of mind that the sales price reflects the actual value of the home. I have seen this technique used to avoid haggling, and come to a fair price for both parties.

Hiring a real estate appraiser will cost a few hundred dollars. But this is an example of money spent that will give a good return. Knowing the current and true market value of the property is an essential step in the marketing process, and you absolutely cannot get the top market value for your property without this. This is money well spent if you are selling as a for-sale-by-owner.

Don't trust an internet evaluation.

Even with knowing every single transaction that occurs, the internet is completely unable to provide proper pricing on real estate. If it could, appraisers and real estate agents would have all been out of business years ago.

You need boots on the ground to know the real value of the property. You need someone who knows the market details such as the current market inventory. You need someone who previews property consistently. The internet doesn't do any of that, and that is why internet price estimates are consistently inaccurate.

To properly market your property, you must know the true market value of the property. There is no way around this, it must be done by a professional. Choose the method of professionally evaluating the property that best suits you, and then get that analysis.

Chapter 14

KNOW YOUR DEMOGRAPHICS

A key element in your marketing plan is to understand the demographics of people who are most likely to buy your product – your real estate.

If you were to leaf through the pages of the latest *Seventeen* magazine, you are unlikely to find an advertisement for denture polish, but you are likely to find an advertisement for make-up. This is an example of marketing to a demographic. Denture polish companies are sure to lose money advertising in *Seventeen* magazine, but make-up companies are more likely to benefit from it.

The same is true when selling real estate. Just as these example products had to know what demographic was likely to buy their product for their marketing plan, so too do you for your product.

First, you must research the current demographic of your neighbourhood.

Very often the people that will be most interested in buying your property will be similar to the people that already live there.

What is the age distribution in your area? Is it an area more with young people or with the elderly?

What is the typical family composition in your area? Is it made up more of single-person households? Childless families? Empty-nesters? Families with children?

What is the average income in the area? This could be a factor in price setting.

What is the employment rate?

What is the ownership percentage in the area? If the ownership rate is low in the neighbourhood, it might do better to market the property more to those who want a rental property. If the ownership percentage is high, it might do better to market it more to prospective homeowners.

What local features will appeal to different demographics?

Different features will be appealing to some demographics but will not interest others. The same features that appeal to one demographic might be a deterrent for others.

Access to transit, as an example, can be a feature that appeals to some but will turn away others. Wealthier communities, as an example, are less likely to be interested in access to public transit, and may even want to stay away from it as they associate it with noise and pollution without any benefit to themselves.

What are the other local amenities?

Good schools, playgrounds, and daycares are features that would lead towards marketing towards families.

A nearby university would likely be best marketed to students, to professors, young professionals, or investors looking to buy a property to rent out to them.

Look at the local amenities, and look at the demographics that frequent those amenities. That same demographic could be who will be most interested in your property.

This isn't to say that your home buyer will fall within that demographic. That isn't the case at all. It could be completely different. But knowing the most likely buyer gives you the edge in your marketing plan in terms of how you present the property, and where your advertising will have the best effect.

What is the highest and best use of the property?

While your property might be a single-family detached residence currently, perhaps that isn't the highest and best use of the property. Perhaps it would be best served to destroy the current improvements and rebuild as a multi-family residence; or as a commercial property; or a mixed-use property.

The only way to know this is to first know the zoning for the area. If the area isn't zoned for multi-family residences then that is not the highest and best use available for it.

Once the zoning is known, then you need to evaluate the different options that could be done with your real estate and see the viability and likelihood of a buyer choosing to invest the capital in using the property as such.

If that is likely, then you have a good idea of how you want to market the property, and where you want to focus your marketing. A property that would only be worth $200,000.00 being used as it currently is could be worth $500,000.00 used differently.

I had a client once that was looking to build a multi-family rental property. We found a property that was currently a single-family rental property but it was in the area he wanted.

My client got a great deal and paid far less than it was worth. He was able to tear down the building and build a new property with multiple units, which the zoning allowed. Being right next to the University, he had no fear that he would ever have trouble finding multiple renters for a steady stream of income.

Had the seller of that house known the highest and best use of that property, they could have marketed it more specifically for that use, gained more attention than they did, and sold it at a higher price than they got. Their mistake benefited my client, but that same mistake won't benefit you as a seller.

To have the best marketing plan, you need to know who will be your most likely buyer. You must learn the current demographic as well as the most likely use of the property and the area around it. You must know your demographics.

SECTION THREE

LIST THE PROPERTY

Chapter 15

SET THE ASKING PRICE

You already know what the value of the property is by following the previous steps. Knowing the value, what should we set as the price?

Some people have a strategy of setting the asking price a good amount above the value because they want to have negotiating room. That sounds fair enough, and there is a logic to it. But it is a method that will usually net a lower final sales price, not a higher one.

Don't set the price too high above the estimated value.

If you set the price too high above the estimated value, you will likely end with a lower final sales price than if you hadn't. There are multiple reasons for this.

Overpriced properties get less advertising exposure.

Fewer people will even see your advertisement if you set the price high. Most people looking to buy a house use a search program and set the maximum price to the maximum price they are willing to spend. They set that as their maximum because there isn't much point in looking for a house that is outside of your price range.

If you set your price at just 4% higher than what it is worth, people looking for houses in the caliber that yours is in will not even see it. For example, if your house is worth $400,000 but you set the price at 4% higher at $416,000, the people who are looking at $400,000 or less won't have your house show up in the list of their search. If fewer people even see the ad, they certainly don't come to view the property.

Overpriced properties get less interest from those that do find it.

The people who will see the ad are those that have a higher budget. But those people won't be interested in your property either. They are looking for a class of property that a higher budget affords. The overpriced house is now competing against better houses, and will again have much less interest generated. Why would someone looking for a house worth $416,000 be interested in a house worth $400,000 that's asking $416,000? They wouldn't. They'll be interested in the houses that seem worth the price.

If your competition prices their properties right, and you price yours high, your competition will get all the interest, and you will get the scraps.

Overpriced houses increase the appeal of the neighbouring houses for sale.

If your property has a reasonably similar value as the nearby houses – which they usually do – then if your house is overpriced, it will just make those other houses look like a bargain. It will increase the interest those houses get – at the expense of yours.

But it also makes houses that are worth more than yours look good, as well. Those houses will have a closer asking price than yours but will be of a higher quality. If your house is worth $400,000 but you're asking $416,000, then the houses that are truly worth $416,000 and are asking in that range will look so much better.

Overpriced properties tend to get fewer offers.

In addition to having fewer people even come to see the property, fewer of those will bother to make an offer.

Here's why.

If you are looking for a property in the $400,000 range, and the property in question seems to be about that quality but is asking $416,000.00, what is a potential buyer likely to do? If they know the true value of the house, and they likely will because over 90% of them will be represented by a real estate agent, then they know it's being overpriced by a whole $16,000.00.

Many buyers won't bother putting in an offer. They won't put in an offer over the value of the house. Indeed, why should they? Why pay more than it's worth?

They won't put in an offer at what the actual value is. The reason for that is they know since the seller has inflated the price, they likely won't accept that offer, and will counter with another offer that is also over the value of the house.

And they often won't put in an offer that's even less than the value. That part seems odd to some home sellers. Why won't they offer less to get the negotiation process going?

Because they often feel that the best way to get the final purchase price around what the house is actually worth is to offer no more than double the difference between the asking price and the value. So if the asking price is $16,000.00 over the value, they have to offer $32,000.00 below the asking price. Their theory in this situation is they want to have a final purchase price that is at or below the value of the house. The only way they feel they can do that is to offer a price where you can 'split the difference' and come to the final price where it should be.

The problem is that many buyers feel that is impolite, and they don't 'want to offend' the seller. Some buyers don't like the negotiation process. They want something that is at the right value from the start. So their answer is just to not bother with an offer and to move on to the next house. It's not like there aren't other houses all over the place for sale.

Overpriced properties will take longer to sell, and risk becoming a stale property.

They say time is money, and there are fewer places where that is truer than with real estate. If you want your house to sell for the top dollar, you don't want it to take too long to sell.

If a house has been on the market longer than the typical days on market at the time, buyers will inevitably ask one question: 'What's wrong with the house?'

Since other houses are selling faster than this house is, there must be something wrong with the house that has kept other people from buying it. The same question comes up if the same property has been on the market, then taken off the market, then put back on the market again.

This is called a 'stale property'. Stale properties have a stigma that they are not as good properties as the others around them – the properties that actually sold. It isn't always a fair or true stigma. One of the biggest causes of a property going stale is that it wasn't marketed properly, and therefore didn't get the exposure needed.

But the fact is that stale properties have that stigma. So they again, don't get as much interest. Fewer buyers are even interested in looking at it than they are for non-stale properties. Fewer buyers put in an offer. And if you get an offer, it doesn't tend to be at the best price you could have gotten if the house hadn't gone stale.

This, of course, is a feedback loop. The staleness of the property decreases interest, which makes it go even staler.

A buyer's agent dealing with his client will usually advise a more aggressive entry into negotiations with a stale property. They know it isn't getting interest. They know they don't have much competition. So if they don't have competition, why pay full price? Also, if the property is vacant, they know the property is bleeding money for the sellers. The sellers still have to pay the taxes, utilities, and insurance on the property, and maybe even a mortgage. So every month this doesn't sell costs the sellers a few hundred to a few thousand dollars.

The seller of such a property will just be losing more and more money if they don't sell it. And the property becomes staler and staler – meaning they will get a smaller purchase price - as time goes on. That gives the advantage to the buyer. So with such a strong entry point for negotiation, the buyers can afford to give very low offers, and they don't need to increase that offer much during negotiation.

The end result of all this is a property that takes longer to sell and sells for a lower price – neither of which benefits you, the seller.

Overpriced properties tend to get low-ball offers.

Fewer buyers put offers on overpriced real estate. And those few that do tend to offer low ball offers if they think it is overpriced. Over 90% of home buyers use a real estate agent, and a skilled real estate agent will be able to estimate the value of the property their client wants to buy and will present them with a CMA before they ever put in an offer. That CMA will show them the real value of that property.

As stated above, when dealing with an overpriced house, the only strategy to enter a negotiation is to offer a very, very low ball offer. Unless they want to pay more than the property is worth, of course. The problem is, no buyer ever really wants to do that.

You also start getting a different type of buyer. You move more into the 'investor' buyers when your house is stale. This is the group of buyers whose sole purpose for their real estate transactions is to buy properties below their market value.

That is not what you want as the seller.

But investors know a stale property doesn't always have anything wrong with it, but they also know it will not likely sell at market value. So they smell blood in the water now and move in for a purchase. The problem is, as the property gets staler and staler, you don't tend to get offers other than from these investors.

If a property is only getting only low offers, or no offers at all, despite it being well marketed, that is often a sign that the asking price is too high above the actual value.

Overpriced properties often have to settle with a low-ball offer.

If a property isn't getting as much exposure as the market would otherwise give, if it isn't getting many offers, and if the only offers it gets are low ball offers, then that property is usually going to have to settle for that lower price, simply because that's the best they are getting.

This is why overpriced properties don't tend to sell for more; they tend to sell for less.

Experienced real estate agents know this. Sometimes they will keep quiet about this fact because they want to make sure they get the listing. Sometimes an agent will inform their client about what is likely to happen but will go along with the overprice because sometimes that's the only way a home seller will come to accept that advice. But doing so does hurt the final purchase price. So it's a lesson that comes with bruising.

The best solution isn't to price it high, or low, but to price it right.

Once you know the value of the house, you also know what you want the price to be – because they should be about the same number.

There are a few exceptions that are some sales tricks in real estate, and other retail sales as well, actually.

You can have a small buffer for 'negotiating room'.

After all that talk against putting negotiating room into the price, I'll let you know you can put in a buffer. A small, small buffer. Generally, keep that buffer around 1% of the value. There are some times when you can go above 1%, which we will discuss below, but they aren't common.

Make sure you also look at the prices of the competition before you add a buffer. If they are priced right, you had better be, too. (The good news is they often aren't)

Keep the asking price under key price points.

People searching for real estate usually search based on key price points that are in blocks of $5,000 or $10,000.

What I mean by that is they will set their search for houses under $415,000. That means houses priced at $415,001 won't even show up in their search parameters. So you want to be aware of that habit of buyers and price your property accordingly.

This means that if your house is worth $397,000, you don't want to add that 1% buffer I mentioned above. If you did, your asking price would be $400,970. You just put yourself outside of the searching block where you will get more views. But an asking price of $399,900 could still fit.

Use 'odd pricing' to price the property by the hundreds, not by the thousands.

A property asking $300,000.00 will get less interest than a house priced at $299,900, even though they are almost exactly the same price. One property lowered the price by just $100, but consumers will often think of a price as being lower than it actually is when odd pricing is utilized. Many people know about this trick, but even when they know about it, it still affects purchasing decisions. So use odd pricing with your real estate asking price.

However, stick to the hundreds. The same house asking $299,999.99 makes this very obvious, and that makes buyers think twice. Buyers know this trick, and they will even accept this trick – but only if it doesn't look too garish.

Check out what your competition is charging.

You want to know what the competition is charging.

The good news is, they usually charge too much. Most sellers want to have a massive buffer in negotiating room, so they overprice their product. Some of them aren't thinking like this is a business transaction, so they didn't price the house at what the market will pay, but at how valuable the house is to them personally.

Overpriced houses are great for you! Since you priced yours right, those houses make yours look even better.

But some houses will be priced aggressively, and you need to have a strategy in mind. If a house is priced very low, don't bother competing with it. It will be gone soon anyway. And this book isn't about how to have a race to the bottom price for your home sale, it's about how to get the top net dollar you can get in your sale.

Then there are the houses that are priced right. This is the most challenging competition for a home seller. The overpriced houses will help your sale. The under-priced will have a negative effect, but only slightly(unless all the houses in the area are like this for some reason). The well-priced houses, though, will be your serious competition.

You want to play with your asking price to push your strengths. Can you adjust your pricing to have a better price per square foot while still being slightly higher? If you're looking at the current market, that means they will be on the market longer than yours has been. Can you adjust the price to be just under their price?

If many properties are all well priced, the next trick might give you an edge.

Avoid 'price banding'.

When sellers are pricing their products, they will have to look at their competition and see what price they are asking. This is also true in real estate.

The consequence is often that they choose a similar price to all the other similar products and so there is a band of options all with the same price.

One trick in selling is to emphasize what makes your product unique. In real estate, this can be both easy and difficult. It's easy because the reality is no two properties are the same. It's difficult because, while not exactly the same, there is a massive ability to substitute one property for another.

But when you see price banding, that gives an opportunity to make your product stand out, and to make it seem more unique than it really is, without doing anything to the property itself. You simply price it differently.

If there are a bunch of properties in the area asking $390,000, and a bunch also asking $410,000, but there are a few asking $400,000, you can make your property stand out by focusing on that price point. Of course, we'll use odd pricing as above, so the asking price is now $399,900.

This is a situation where you can get away with increasing your 'negotiating room' to beyond 1%. But you still can't get carried away. This trick can give you an edge, but you can lose that edge if you push it too far. Also, this trick only works if there is banding pricing both below and above a price point that is otherwise vacant.

Don't be too worried about underpricing your property.

If you have to err on one side of the coin, either over-pricing or under-pricing your property, you are unquestionably better off with under-pricing it. Hands down.

Over-priced properties don't get much interest. So they rarely sell at even market value.

Under-priced properties do tend to get more interest. So they are more likely to get multiple bidders – which tends to increase the final purchase price.

I had some clients once who were looking to buy a house. When searching for them, I found one in their area that needed a good amount of work, but its bones were good. So this property isn't showing well, but it has value and just needed some sweat equity to make it a steal of a deal.

This property had just come on the market that morning. It was asking $340,000, but I estimated the value at $380,000 in its current condition and over $420,000 if they cleaned the place up, and made some easy, minor repairs – repairs that wouldn't cost that additional $40,000.

My clients could only go up to $360,000 and pay for the repairs expected. That was the most they could afford. I recommended that they put in an offer for $360,000, a full $20,000 more than the asking price.

It takes a lot of faith for people to listen to their agent when he says to offer $20,000 higher than the asking price. But these clients trusted me and they made that offer.

They still lost. We didn't get the house. It sold that very day for $380,000.

This story shows how underpricing has a safety net. That safety net is that more and more people will see the house, and will be interested. They won't likely get into a bidding war that will pay more than the house is worth. But they could get into a bidding war bringing the price up to market value.

Now, imagine if that house had asked for $40,000 more than it was worth. No one would have even bothered to see it.

Under-priced properties often sell at more than the asking price. So under-pricing a property can still lead to the house selling at the market price.

This isn't to say that your strategy should be to underprice the property. It shouldn't be. Your strategy should be to follow these pages and price it right. Don't price it too high, don't price it too low – price it right. But don't be too concerned that you priced it too low; that problem is often self-corrected by the increased interest. Be more concerned about overpricing. Overpricing doesn't have that same ability to self-correct; it just costs you.

If you price the house right, you get the most interest, the most offers, and the best offers. If you overprice the property, you are less likely to sell the house at the highest market value. You are more likely to sell it at a discount. Price it right the first time for the best results, and the most money in your pocket.

Chapter 16

DECIDE WHAT STAYS AND WHAT GOES

Generally speaking in real estate, everything that is attached to the property is considered to be included in the sale without specifying it in the purchase contract. Things that are not attached to the property are considered to not be included in the sale unless specified in the purchase contract.

This means that a chandelier and other light fixtures will be considered to be included in the purchase without being mentioned in the contract.

The oven, however, will not be considered as included. It will have to be listed if it forms part of the purchase – which they usually do.

When you are making your listing, you should think about the attached goods that you might not want to include in the purchase. If you wanted to keep a chandelier, for example, then you should take steps to do so when you are making the listing.

One option is to remove the attached goods you want to keep. If they aren't attached when you are showing the home and the contract is made, then this isn't an issue.

Another option is simply to list some exclusions in your listing and then specify those exclusions again in the purchase contract.

Don't forget that step. It doesn't matter if the item was listed as an exclusion in the listing if it also isn't excluded in the purchase contract. It's the purchase contract that will be enforceable.

Also, list all the items that you have that are not attached that are staying. This is usually comprised of the appliances. Again, make sure they are all also specified in the purchase contract.

Chapter 17

Be Upfront About Defects and List Them

Do not try to sell real estate without being upfront and honest about any material latent defects in the house. In a sense, all properties will have defects of some sort. You don't have to list them all. But you do have to specifically disclose any material latent defects.

For a defect to be a material latent defect it must meet a few qualifications.

1 – It must be material - it must matter. A defect is material when reasonable people would agree it is significant in the particular circumstances of a transaction.

2 – It must be latent – it must be not-easily discoverable. A defect is latent if it cannot be discovered with reasonable care during an inspection.

So that spells out the defects in the property that you must disclose. If you have a hole in the ceiling in the middle of the room, you do not need to disclose that. This is because while most people would agree that problem is material, most people would agree it matters; it is also easily discoverable, so it isn't latent.

Some characteristics of what would make a defect material is if it would: make a property dangerous or potentially dangerous; make a property unfit for habitation; or make a property unfit for the buyer's purpose (if the buyer has told the seller their purpose).

Other characteristics would be if: the defect is very expensive to repair; the seller has received a local government or authority notice that a circumstance of the property must be remedied; the seller does not have appropriate building or other permits for the property.

Any latent defect that meets these characteristics would likely be considered material, and therefore would have to be disclosed.

However, this list is not exhaustive. It is impossible to list all the circumstances that could possibly be considered a material, latent defect. In general, you should consult a real estate professional – either a real estate lawyer or a licensed real estate agent.

The last thing you want with your home sale is a lawsuit in a few years.

As a seller, you must disclose to the buyer or the buyer's representative any material latent defects in the property that you know about. Never participate in hiding or disguising known defects.

Chapter 18

Have an Inspection Ready to Give to Potential Buyers

It may seem counter-intuitive, but a seller paying for a home inspection ahead of the property going on the market has many significant advantages.

In many cases, home sellers don't bother with a home inspection. It is left to the home buyer to arrange and pay for the home inspection after they have made an offer to purchase which the seller has accepted.

But some savvy home sellers take it on their own to pay for an inspection before the house is listed. This is called a 'pre-listing inspection'.

Why should home sellers go through that expense?

An inspection gives the seller valuable information on any repairs that need to be made.

With this information, the home seller is better able to assess what renovations need to be done. There may be renovations needed that you aren't aware of. With a proper inspection, you get a more complete picture and can make a more educated decision.

An inspection gives the home seller the ability to adjust the price of the property to reflect any issues before it is listed.

If you have a property for sale at any price, and there is a defect, the home buyers will usually want to have a price reduction.

But you can avoid that if you disclose the issue ahead of time. Then you can reasonably state that the issue is already reflected in the price and there is no reason to reduce it further.

If you don't disclose the issues ahead of time, then this argument doesn't usually succeed in assuaging the concerns of the home buyer.

An inspection gives the home seller confidence in the real value of the home.

Knowing the condition of the property after it is inspected gives the home seller confidence that they are not selling a lemon. That confidence translates into more negotiating power.

An inspection reduces the risk of an unforeseen issue undermining the sale process.

Imagine that you worked hard to sell the property. You decluttered, cleaned, and did all the renovations you thought were needed.

Then you went through the hard work of marketing and showing the property.

Then you went through the hard work of negotiating a sales agreement subject to an inspection for the buyer.

Only then to have the buyer come back to re-negotiate the sale with a lower purchase price because of some issue their inspection found.

Unless that issue was already disclosed, they will then say 'Our offer price was based on the understanding the house was in good condition. This issue means the house price should be lowered so we can correct it.'

The last thing you want at this stage is to re-negotiate the price. You're less able to fall back on other interested parties at this stage than you are before you sign a sales agreement. Before the property is pending, you may well have other interested parties that can step in if one offer goes south. But at this stage, there are usually no other interested parties willing to stay in line for your property for a few weeks while it is pending.

The excitement and newness of the house being for sale are also diminished at this point. While it might not yet be stale, it is certainly not as fresh as it was.

Most often, if a buyer finds an issue that wasn't known before the offer, the best choice is to re-negotiate. But we don't want to do that. So having an inspection is a good means to reduce that risk.

If a home buyer tries to lower the price due to an issue on their inspection, the home seller can rightly state that this issue was already known to the buyer before the purchase agreement. There is then no legitimate reason to lower the agreed price.

Potentially save the cost of the inspection for your buyer.

By having the home inspection already done and available to the buyer, the purchase of your property saves them time and money.

That is something that might help your property stand out among all the others.

Demonstrates that you are forthcoming in disclosures.

Sometimes there is something in a property that isn't known to both the seller and the buyer. Sometimes the buyer would seek damages for the issue.

In this case, the seller could claim they didn't know, but if it is only their word, then there could be a doubt that it is true.

By providing a pre-listing inspection, the home seller can now state that they made every attempt to locate and disclose all issues by hiring a professional inspector and providing that inspection to all prospective buyers. It now becomes more difficult for any buyer to claim that the seller was knowingly selling a property that had material latent defects.

However, this does not absolve the sellers of the responsibility to honestly disclose any material latent defects. If there are any known, they should be shared with the inspector and included in the inspection report.

Pre-listing inspections can make for a faster close.

During a very hot seller's market, it isn't uncommon for buyers to skip the inspection because they know that time is very limited, and they want to get an accepted offer.

But this also leaves them with an uneasy feeling. That uneasy feeling means they are not going to be as enthusiastic about price.

Having the inspection done and ready for them means they can feel better about presenting an offer to purchase without an inspection condition.

That means you could potentially get more simultaneous offers, and get a more pronounced bidding war for your property.

Don't object to the buyers getting their own inspection as well.

During a very hot seller's market, you might get half to two-thirds of buyers willing to go without an inspection. In that case, they will gladly use yours.

But during a balanced or buyer's market, fewer home buyers are going to forego an inspection despite you having provided one already.

In all cases, simply tell the sellers that you conducted an inspection to assess the condition of the property before listing it; and that you are more than happy to share it with them; but they are also free to get their own inspection done.

Do this and buyers will feel confident that they have a choice and that everything is upfront with the property.

It isn't the usual practice of home sellers to provide an inspection for buyers. But having a pre-listing inspection gives many advantages to the seller, even if it ultimately isn't relied upon by the buyer.

Chapter 19

WRITE UP A LIST OF FEATURES & BENEFITS

To help focus on what will entice your prospective buyer, it's best to make a list of the features and benefits of your property. But to do that, we first need to understand the difference between features and benefits from a marketing point of view.

When writing marketing copy there are two approaches. One is to list the things that the product is or does. The second is to focus on how that will benefit the reader. The best sales copy creates an emotional response in the reader; it makes them want the product. That means focusing on benefits.

Features are the facts about the property – such as having a high-efficiency furnace, for example.

Benefits are how the features improve the life of the reader – such as saving money with that high-efficiency furnace.

They are very closely related concepts and the truth is most copywriters have difficulty mastering this. But despite the difficulty, the fact of the matter is products are sold by benefits, not features. So that's what we want to focus on.

The easiest way to start that process is just to list the features. Don't worry about the benefits at this point. That's because people tend to have no issue listing the features. That's easy. They have difficulty in expressing the benefit. So start with a list of the features.

List everything that you think is a selling point. Write down the features that you love about the house. Here are some common features.

1 – It has a garage. Write down the type. How many cars can fit? Is it attached or detached?

2 – Type of flooring.

3 – Height of ceiling

4 – Type of bathrooms, and how many. Is one an ensuite bathroom attached to the master bedroom?

5 – A gourmet kitchen.

6 – Theatre room.

7 – Home office.

8 – Walk-in closets

9 – Fireplace

10 – Upgraded countertops – Granite, quartz, etc.

11 – Home gym

It might be that your property doesn't have many of these. That's ok. There's a market for your type of property. It doesn't need to have all these features to be able to sell. Still, think about the features your property does have. What do you love about it? Write those features down.

Make sure to include any good, unique features of your property.

A common and successful strategy in marketing is to have a Unique Selling Point (USP). The USP is something that sets your product apart from the other products around. It doesn't have to be lavish, or expensive – it just has to be different and to have some sort of benefit (explained below).

So if there's something unique about your property, but it doesn't add a benefit, then it isn't a good choice for a USP. The good news is if your unique element just looks good that is beneficial enough to include when selling real estate.

Another reason to make sure any USPs you have are included in the write-up and photographs is it helps distinguish your property from the others and helps to keep it in mind. Buyers will often see a dozen or two houses before they put in an offer. Eventually, they often start to merge their memories and can't remember one house from another. This means some houses get forgotten, and even if they were otherwise good houses they don't make the shortlist. Highlighting the unique aspects of your property helps to reduce that effect for your property, and that means it stays more in the minds of buyers.

Write out the benefits of your property's features.

Now that you've written down the list of features, it's time to write down what those benefits are.

The most common benefits used in advertising are: saves time, peace of mind, saves money, makes money, convenience, fun, and self-image.

Generally speaking, all benefits fall into those categories.

So go through the list of features you have, and see which one(s) of these benefits fit each feature.

Match the benefits to the buyer.

This is where knowing your demographic comes into play. Are you selling a luxury, executive estate home? Then you probably don't even want to mention that there's an LRT station around the corner.

Think about each benefit and think about which ones would be most appealing to your target demographic. Those are the features and benefits that you should focus on.

Now you're ready to start writing good advertising copy.

Chapter 20

WRITE AN ADVERTISEMENT THAT SELLS

Now that you know who your target demographic is, and you have a list of the benefits to appeal to that demographic, it's time to write up a killer advertisement that really sells this property.

This is a stage that often separates the marketing pros from the amateurs. It isn't an easy thing to do to write up a good real estate advertisement, and that's why most of them aren't good. This isn't an easy thing to do. Few people are good copywriters, and the best copywriters can charge six figures for one piece of copy. That fact alone should tell you how important and effective good copy is.

People often find themselves staring at a blank page for a long time without any idea of what to even start writing. This includes some professional real estate agents. Sometimes they just repeat the details of the property that's already in the specifications. "3BR/2Bath Condo for sale" That's it? That's the whole ad? That isn't going to show why people should choose your property over all the other 3 bedroom, 2 bathroom condos around. Don't do that.

Don't copy everyone else.

Most real estate ads aren't very good. So don't look at what everyone else is doing and do the same thing here. Sometimes that's a good strategy in life – here it isn't.

Know the AIDA formula, and use it.

AIDA is a marketing acronym that stands for:

Attention - Interest - Desire - Action

AIDA is the formula used as the industry standard in marketing and advertising. It is a description of the steps that best lead not only to someone reading the advertising – but then to the highest success in the reader also buying the product.

Grab the *attention* of the reader.

You need to capture this in either the headline or the first sentence if there isn't a headline (as there often isn't in real estate ads). If there isn't a headline, treat the first sentence like the headline and it will achieve the same results.

The first step in writing a good headline is to answer these questions:

Who is your customer? This goes back to knowing your target demographic, and why that knowledge is so critical.

What are the important features of the product? (Features)

Why would your customer want to buy a product that has your features? (Benefits)

Now that we have those in place, we can start writing the headline. There are two related rules in writing the headline for your copy: the 80% rule and the 50/50 rule.

The 80% rule says that 80% of the success of an advertisement comes from the headline. So getting the first step right is crucial. Everything else is there to reinforce and support your headline. You often don't have much room here, so you have to make every word count. Prefer a short, descriptive headline.

The 50/50 rule is that since the headline is so important, 50% of the time you spend writing the advertising copy should be focused on the headline. It's that important. The other 50% is spent on all the rest.

A good headline also follows "the four u's". They should be unique, ultra-specific, create a sense of urgency, and be useful.

Be unique – the first 'u'.

Even if you were selling the exact same product as your competition, one way to distinguish your product is just to have a unique headline. The writing itself helps create uniqueness, and uniqueness sells. If you sound the same as everyone else, there is no way you can also be grabbing attention. So being unique is the key. Don't get too worried about this. If other copywriters in the area are also unique, that doesn't mean you're not. Just don't write the exact same thing they do.

That said, it's even better if your product is unique and the writing is also. That's a killer combination. So focus on the unique features of your property. One nice thing about real estate is that even though real estate is considered a commodity, it is also unique. No two properties are alike, and they never can be. So one easy way to add some uniqueness is to mention the neighbourhood. A nice benefit to this is that it also grabs the attention of people who are looking for that neighbourhood. This is best used in desirable neighbourhoods, but it doesn't hurt anywhere. There's no point hiding where the property is. People are going to find out anyway.

You don't need to focus as much on the feature vs benefit issue in the headline (Unless you have room to, which would be great!).

Be ultra-specific, the second 'u'.

It should be terse; short and sweet. You can only measure this in a few words, not long sentences. So there is no room for wasted space. An ultra-specific headline doesn't have a single word that isn't needed.

Very often the headline, or your first sentence, will be written with 'newspaper language'. Think 'The President Saved a Dog' in a newspaper headline. It's never written like that. They don't follow the usual grammatical rules for a complete sentence. Instead, they will read 'President Saves Dog'. For your headline, follow the same rules. Usually, omit any "the" or "a". That's a waste of space that you don't want.

Be ruthless. Delete anything that doesn't add value to the headline.

What's best is to have it filled with multi-purpose words that both create a sense of urgency and usefulness – the next two u's.

Create a sense of urgency – the third 'u'.

It isn't easy to create a sense of urgency and be terse at the same time. In fact, it isn't always possible in the headline, but if it can be incorporated it should be.

One way to create a sense of urgency is to create a sense of scarcity. Express that this is a unique house and/or a limited-time opportunity for the buyer. Buyers act more emotionally and more readily when they feel that they will lose out if the chance for their gain is limited.

As you can see that's hard to do in only a few words. But there are a few tricks. Here are some words to throw into a headline that create urgency:

Hurry	Wow	Call Now	Won't Last
Rare	Unique	Don't Wait	Don't Miss This
Act Now	New	Quick	

The "Call Now" is a nice one that also includes an action – which is never a bad thing.

Of course, only use the words above that best describe the subject property. If the property isn't particularly rare or unique, don't use those words. If the property is over-priced, don't use "Won't last", because if the property is on the market for a while, the "won't last" seems untrue – and as soon as a reader thinks a part of the ad is untrue, they also think the rest will be, too.

Mentioning how your product can solve a problem or relieve a stress of your reader is also an excellent way to build urgency. This also has the good side effect of being useful, which is the next piece of the puzzle.

Be useful – the final 'u' of a headline.

Does your headline suggest that if they bothered to read the actual body of the ad that it would be useful to them?

The headline needs to suggest to the reader that your product could be the solution to their problem. If your headline suggests that it solves the problem, then the reader has a good reason to keep reading and get more details. The good news is that if you've done the other 3 steps right, this step is usually already answered.

You can't always get all 4 u's in your headline. That's just a reality. But your goal in the copywriting for the headline is to pack as many of them in it as you can.

One last tip in making a headline – ask a question.

Not every headline should be a question, of course; but asking a question is a time-tested way to create some interest in a headline. When people read a question, they often answer it in their thoughts and often want to read a bit to either learn the answer or even to see if what is written agrees with their own answer. Don't overdo questions in headlines, but do keep them in your toolkit.

Build interest in your product.

Now that you have their attention, you need to keep them reading and guide them down the buying process highlighting why your product is the right solution for their needs.

You only have between 5 and 15 seconds to achieve this. That's how quickly interest fades in most readers of advertisements. So you have to make this work right from the first few sentences. To do this you have to create a sense that this product has tangible and relevant benefits to your potential customer.

From the previous chapter, we know that benefits sell, not features. So the advertising copy has to focus on the benefits.

Newly built home? That's not a benefit, that's a feature. The peace of mind that the house has a long life left, the peace of mind that repairs aren't likely in the near future, or the prestige of owning a newer home are all examples of benefits for that feature.

2500 square feet of space? That's not a benefit, that's a feature. The convenience of having so much space or the prestige of owning a large home are benefits.

New roof? That's a feature. The peace of mind that you don't expect to repair the roof soon, the peace of mind that the house is well maintained, or the self-image of a good looking home with its new roof are all benefits.

New high-efficiency furnace? That's a feature. The money-saving from the lower energy bills, the peace of mind that it won't likely need replacement soon, or the self-image that the owner is being energy conscious are the benefits.

Always sell the benefits, not the features.

Don't just repeat the specs of the property. Everyone can already see that it's a 3 bedroom with 1500 square feet in the property specifications. If you're going to mention anything, you have to anchor it with a benefit (see above).

For example, if you must restate that there is a 3 car garage, don't just repeat that, anchor it with how that benefits the buyer. Don't write '3 car garage'; write 'There's space for all your cars, toys, and tools in the roomy 3 car garage'.

Now they're interested, bring out a *desire* to actually purchase the property.

Create a sense of urgency. Spell out why the property you are selling is an exciting opportunity. Buyers react more to a purchase when it seems like a limited opportunity. That is why we see sales in retail stores for a limited time.

You always want to create the sense of urgency for your property and to show it as an exciting opportunity.

You want every ad to be exciting! If you want the property to sell at top market value you need to show that this home sale is an exciting opportunity for the buyer, and you have to spell out in your ad that they don't want to miss this opportunity.

It doesn't matter what the condition of the property is – it's always a good product, and a great buy. Is your property smaller than others in the neighbourhood? Then it's a bargain. That's a valuable product. Is your property a teardown? That's a product that is a great deal for builders. That's also a valuable product.

Price is a factor here, as well as time on market. If a property has been on the market for too long it will seem less and less like an exciting opportunity – one of many reasons why over-priced homes don't sell for as much money.

An exciting opportunity gets results from buyers.

Don't write 'motivated seller', 'price negotiable', or 'bring offers'.

These phrases are a massive red flag to a buyer that your property is asking a price that is too high, you're desperate to sell, and that they shouldn't give you a good offer. There is no reason to ever write this.

'Motivated seller' translates into desperate to sell.

'Price negotiable' translates into will sell for less than the asking price – so no need to send a good offer.

'Bring offers'. Are there sellers that don't want offers?

All of these phrases, and those like them, send a signal that you don't have a good product, there are no other buyers interested, and that you are desperate to sell. That is exactly the last signal we ever want to send to a buyer. Buyers don't want to buy any property from a desperate seller, that's the exact opposite of an exciting opportunity. And when buyers are willing to put in an offer on what they now see as an overpriced property with a desperate seller, it won't be anywhere near full price.

No matter what the condition of the property, you've set this up to appeal to the right buyer. So you don't ever need to advertise that your product is sub-standard. It never is, it's just got to be marketed to the right buyer.

If you've done the marketing right, you don't need to signal that you have a weak negotiating position right from the start. The price of your property isn't going to be that negotiable, because you've already done your homework and priced it right. That means you're going to get the level of interest that your property deserves at that price point. Of course, if you've overpriced the property this isn't true. This is one of the reasons why it is so important to price the property correctly right from the beginning, and why overpricing leads to lower final sale prices.

Signalling from the beginning that your home is overpriced and that you want to unload it will not get you the top market value. If you are in a position where you must sell quickly, just price it accordingly from the start. That gets eyeballs on your property and offers in your inbox – not broadcasting that you have a bad property at a bad price.

Chapter 21

GET PROFESSIONAL PHOTOGRAPHS, A FLOOR PLAN, AND A 3D TOUR

This is a critical stage – the photographs. Do not go cheap on this part. Expect to pay a few hundred dollars by hiring a professional real estate photographer.

Having poor photographs is a major disservice to your efforts in marketing the property. How can someone expect that they will generate the same amount of interest if they have photographs that don't make the property look as beautiful and appealing as possible? They can't.

I understand the desire to save money and spend as little as possible. In many situations, that's prudent thinking. In this book, I've written about not spending money where it won't benefit the sale many times. This, however, is not one of those situations.

This is a point where you want to spend – with one exception. If you are not able to get the property well maintained, clean, and essentially move-in ready; then you can reduce this expense. If you don't have much to showcase in terms of looks because the property needs maintenance or cleaning, then there's no point in spending the extra money. Sometimes a property can be at a stage where you don't even want any interior photographs at all. I have sold some properties like that when they were either dilapidated or filthy. Photos in those cases wouldn't only not help the sale, they would actually hinder it.

If your property is well maintained and clean, then definitely don't skip on this. It doesn't matter how old the property is. If it's old, there is a market available of people that like quaint. It doesn't matter how small it is. There's a market for that. Really, the only reason to not get good photos is if it isn't well maintained and clean.

Choose a high-quality real estate photographer.

You don't need to break the bank, but you also don't want to be cheap here. You will get what you pay for with real estate photography. You want someone who is experienced with this specific type of photography.

Top-quality real estate photographers will be able to take a wide dynamic range in their photographs so that there are no shadows or bright areas that obscure the details.

They will take care in having vertical lines that don't converge. They will use the right angle of lens that makes the property look as spacious as the human eye would see it if you were in the room.

What you want are photos that are accurate but also having the property looking its best.

Don't get photos that make the rooms seem bigger than they actually are.

Transparency is key. While you definitely will get more interest if the photos make the property seem bigger, you will also disappoint the people that do come to the property and that initial interest will fade. Additionally, it makes you seem dishonest. Once buyers think you are dishonest in one aspect of the sale, they will always have it in the back of their mind asking if you are dishonest elsewhere.

Get an accurate floor plan made.

This is something developers do very well, and home sellers should pay attention.

Buyers love to see a floor plan. It gives them real insight into the structure of the house and they can already begin to imagine what that house would be like to live in. That's exactly the mindset we want to put in our potential buyers.

Get a 3D Tour of the property.

The technology that is available now for sellers to be able to showcase their homes to everyone is amazing, and sellers should be taking advantage of this.

Again, this is a service that costs a few hundred dollars typically. But it's also a service where that expense is justified. Like above with photographs, skip this step if the property is not well maintained or clean.

Giving buyers the option to look over the actual property in a virtual 3D tour helps buyers decide if the property is what they want before they even see it in person. If the property isn't what they want, then they don't waste your time in a viewing. If the property is what they want, then they come to the viewing already more likely to buy it because they've already decided this property meets their needs.

Chapter 22

List the Property on the MLS®

The MLS® is the Multiple Listing Service that is used by REALTOR® associations. Real estate brokerages that are members of those associations can list their properties for sale on this system. As a result, their properties will display not only on their websites but on the websites for all other brokerages that are also members. This greatly increases the internet marketing available to sell properties. Rather than appear on one or two websites, the property appears on hundreds or even thousands of websites.

So it is quite easy to see how advantageous it is to be listed on the MLS® system.

There is a time and place to not use the MLS®.

Under rare circumstances, sellers want to avoid using the MLS®. The most common cause is that they don't want their home sale to be made public. They want it to be low-key.

That usually isn't a strategy that brings about the best purchase price. In fact, it all but guarantees you won't get the best price. But those sellers prefer privacy over getting the highest return.

Some sellers also don't want to ever have any real estate agents involved in the real estate transaction. They don't want a real estate agent representing them or the buyers. Listing on the MLS® again all but guarantees that the buyer will be represented by a real estate agent. However, 90% of buyers are represented by a real estate agent anyway. So this isn't a method to guarantee the buyer won't be represented.

Properties on the MLS® give the contact information for the brokerage website, not the seller or the seller's brokerage.

This is the part that many for sale by owners miss. When you list your home on the MLS®, that means your property will show up on the websites of all the real estate brokerages belonging to that real estate association. But they are doing that to help their buyers buy a home with their help. They aren't giving free advertising to anyone. So the contact information on their websites isn't to the seller or the seller's brokerage. It's to themselves.

So while you do get access to hundreds of websites advertising your home being for sale. Interested buyers seeing the home on those websites aren't given your contact information, they are given the information to the owner of those websites – which are real estate brokers.

That isn't a problem, usually. In fact the higher exposure tends to also bring about better offers. But it does mean that if you never want to deal with a real estate agent, using the MLS® is counter-productive.

Only real estate brokerages can access the MLS®.

There's no other way to post a property on the MLS® than to go through a real estate brokerage. REALTORS® own the MLS® system, and only they can use it.

But you can pick a brokerage that has the price you want.

It is illegal for REALTORS® to collude together to all have the same price to access the MLS®. There is also an abundance of competition in the real estate industry. This means there are as many different price structures as you can probably imagine.

Keep in mind, while collusion is illegal, it is perfectly legal for a real estate brokerage to have a set fee structure, and a set fee amount that every agent in their brokerage must obey, if that brokerage chooses to do so.

Some agents work on commission, and they are only paid after they successfully sell the house. Some agents work with a paid upfront structure, and they are paid before any work is done and it doesn't matter if you sell the house. Some agents will do either type of structure or a hybrid of both.

There are also a variety of services that you can choose.

Some agents use the MLS® with an upfront fee to merely list the property on the MLS® and provide no other services. This is appropriately called a 'mere listing'. Sometimes this is just a few hundred dollars. But the price can be whatever the real estate brokerage chooses to ask for their services.

Some structures provide some services that are typically associated with being represented by an agent, but not every service.

Some structures are 'full service', which provide all the services usually offered by real estate agents. This can be a misnomer, as the agents don't do absolutely everything for you. For example, they don't usually clean your house before every showing. So even with what one might call a 'full service', the services must always be defined.

Those are the multitude of options available to sellers who want to utilize the MLS®. They do have to go through a real estate brokerage, but they can pick and choose which brokerage has the services and prices that they want.

Around 80% of homes sold are through the MLS®.

This figure comes from the National Association of REALTORS®. It demonstrates the power and effectiveness of the system. If this is how 80% of homes are sold and have been for decades, there is good reason why this is remaining so effective.

The MLS® system is very effective in increasing exposure to your property. There are many different types of services that can give you MLS® access, and at many different price structures, but they are all through real estate brokerages that are members of their local real estate association. Using the MLS®, by merit of the additional exposure alone, is likely to increase your likelihood of getting an offer, and to increase the likelihood of getting a higher offer.

Unless you have specific reasons that you don't want your property sale to be made so public, I highly recommend you use the MLS® system in your real estate sale.

SECTION FOUR

MARKET THE PROPERTY

Chapter 23

Know the Difference Between 'Passive' and 'Active' Marketing

One might wonder why after having so much time devoted to listing the property that there is now an entire section on marketing the property. This is because listing the property is not the same as marketing it.

If all it took to sell a house for top value is an MLS listing, internet or paper ads, and a for sale sign, then there would be no need for this book, and real estate agents would have all been out of business decades ago. Just listing the property and putting up a sign and some ads is not a proper marketing strategy. This section is devoted to a comprehensive strategy that the top real estate agents use to now get the home sold.

There are two ways to market anything – passive marketing and active marketing. Passive marketing is advertisements, google search results, lawn signs, etc. It's putting up a display somewhere and waiting for the customer to contact you. Active marketing is going out and finding the customers. It's direct sales, utilizing a sphere of influence, cold calling, etc.

Each of these styles of advertising have advantages and disadvantages, and each of them has their place in real estate. Let's examine the advantages and disadvantages of passive and active marketing in general.

Advantages of passive marketing:

1 – It is less labour intensive. It doesn't involve nearly as much work and effort.

2 – It doesn't require a well-established network of contacts relevant to real estate.

3 – It is cheaper compared to paying someone to do the labour of active marketing (It's more expensive than doing the labour of the active marketing yourself though, which can cost more time than money).

4 – It doesn't require specialized know how. Pretty much anyone can put up signs and classified ads.

5 – You don't need strong interpersonal or networking skills.

Disadvantages of passive marketing:

1 – It takes a long time to get results. Passive marketing works better for a long-term campaign than it does for a short-term marketing campaign. That means passive marketing can achieve results well for a business that plans to stay in business for years on end. But that isn't what a home seller wants. They don't want to be marketing the property for years, they want to sell it. So an active marketing campaign will yield better results.

2 - Passive marketing alone does not yield the best results in real estate. If it did, there would no longer be any real estate sales industry. If putting up an ad on the MLS, sticking a lawn sign in the front yard, and running a few ads online and in the paper was all it took to sell a house for the top sales price, this industry would have been destroyed decades ago. It does not get the best results in real estate in terms of both speed of sale and final profit margin.

108   Get The Home Sold

The National Associate of Realtors report bears this out. Internet sites, search engines, newspaper ads, Yellow Pages, home magazine ads, and direct mail account for less than 15 percent of all closed buyer leads.

3 – It costs more money than doing active marketing yourself. Passive marketing tends to cost more money in the form of a display. Active marketing tends to cost more in the form of labour and effort.

Advantages of active marketing in real estate:

1 – It gets faster results. Direct marketing doesn't wait for the customer to find the product. It goes right to the customer.

2 – It makes more money. There's a reason that Coca-Cola still employs direct sales agents despite their domination of the market. Direct sales gets results and is very effective.

3 – It's more hands-on and can get a better feel for the market. This gives you a time advantage in responding to what is working and not working in your campaign and changes in the market itself.

Disadvantages of active marketing in real estate:

1 – You have to be a salesperson. Most people don't want to be salespeople, and most people wouldn't be good salespeople. Some people don't even like salespeople. That's fair enough. But good salespeople get results, and active marketing means you're a salesperson.

2 – You have to be outgoing, initiate conversations, and then direct them politely and effectively towards buying your product.

3 – You have to be willing to accept constant rejection. The general rule of thumb is you will get ninety-nine "no's" before you get a "yes". You have to be able to let that rejection slide right off your back.

4 – You need strong interpersonal skills. You are now marketing on a personal level, not an impersonal ad where you don't even

meet the reader. A salesperson with poor interpersonal skills will just annoy people and push away a sale. That's a bad salesperson, of course, and most of us have a negative experience with this.

5 – It is very time-consuming. This is called active marketing for a reason. It takes action – constant action.

6 – You have to know where to spend your time to best reach your customers. Time is money is true here.

7 – You need a pre-established network and sphere of influence with many people that are relevant to the buying and selling of real estate.

So which do you need in real estate?

Optimally, you need both. You want to use passive marketing in conjunction with an active marketing strategy. Passive marketing on its own will simply not generate the same results in most cases.

Most everyone knows how to do passive marketing, so we'll focus more on the active components.

Chapter 24

CONTACT EVERYONE IN THE NEIGHBOURHOOD TO TELL THEM THE PROPERTY IS FOR SALE

It is quite interesting just how many sales you can get by marketing to the specific area of the house for sale. There's a saying in realty that real estate is hyper-local. This is an example of that.

It isn't usually the people in the immediate area that end up buying the house – although that also does happen as a result of hyper-local marketing. But the people in the immediate area are the people who are most likely to know someone who wants to move into that area. This makes them a prime candidate to leverage your marketing.

Don't overlook marketing to the neighbourhood. It can pay off very well.

Install a high-quality, professional lawn sign.

The first stage in marketing to the neighbourhood is of course a professional lawn sign. You do want it to look professional, so a $5 generic sign that you scribble some information on absolutely will not do.

You are serious about selling this property; you want to project seriousness in your sign.

You have not been cheap with the maintenance of the property; you don't want to project cheapness with your sign.

You are concerned about aesthetics in your property; you want to project beauty and sophistication in your sign.

So get a professional lawn sign made, and make sure it looks great – professionally made lawn signs that are tattered are equally unacceptable.

Send 'Just Listed' cards to the neighbours.

Now that your sign is up, continue to leverage the force multiplier of hyper-local real estate marketing by giving the neighbours just listed cards.

This is a mini-advertisement so you want it to stand out, and there are a few ways to do that.

Specify the neighbourhood that you are in. People are more interested in that which is most related to themselves. So when they see things related to themselves – such as their name, or the same model car they drive – they are more likely to give that just a little more attention than otherwise. This same phenomenon works with their neighbourhood name. People are also more interested in the sale of neighbourhood properties because they tend to wonder what the market value of their own home might be.

Have it professionally designed. A well-designed and professionally made postcard stands out. An exceptionally poorly designed postcard will also stand out – but not in a good way that will help you sell the property.

Put a list of your features and benefits on the card.

You don't need all your photos. There's limited space on a postcard, so you need to pick and choose your top 3 photos at most. Kitchens and exteriors are usually winners if you only have

3 photos, but you can use your judgement about which photos you took that are best.

Put the price on the postcard. Most people are too busy or not interested enough just by your postcard to look up the price you are asking. Don't make your potential buyers do more work than they have to – because many of them won't.

Deliver the postcards through mail or door-to-door.

Generally speaking, I usually recommend door-to-door delivery in real estate. Real estate is very much an interpersonal trade that works face to face. If that weren't so then computers and the internet would have already taken over this business decades ago.

However, the 'Just Listed' cards are one that you can get away with sending to the neighbourhood in the mail if you prefer to; but only if you go door-to-door afterwards as well – which we will discuss next.

Do direct door to door marketing.

Everybody hates doing this. For sale by owners don't like doing it. Realtors don't like doing this. Nobody likes doing this.

Do it anyway. It works.

Do this either to deliver the 'Just Listed' postcards above or do it just after you've delivered them.

Delivering the postcards as you go door-to-door will save you the delivery costs. But mailing the postcards and then going door to door means you get another 'touch' on your sales process. Since we know each touch moves a prospective buyer closer towards making a buying decision, having multiple touches means better chances of success.

After you have delivered the 'Just Listed' cards, your objective is to talk to twenty people in the area every single day who are decision-makers in buying real estate. A decision-maker is an adult who is capable of buying real estate in this situation. So adults who cannot buy do not count, and children do not count.

When going door-to-door, expect that you won't be able to talk to anyone at 70% of the houses you knock on. That could be because they aren't home, or they are home and don't want to talk to you. Both of those are fine. Just move on to the next house.

10% of people will answer but won't have time to talk. The vast majority of those people will be very polite about their inability to spend time right now for you. Never press this. If they indicate that they aren't interested, tell them politely about your sale, thank them for their time, and move on.

The other 20% will be people that are willing to politely hear what you have to say.

The objective of going door to door is to interest someone to either buy your property themselves or refer your sale to someone they know who wants to move to the neighbourhood.

One might ask why would someone who lives in the neighbourhood want to buy a house here? There are a few answers. Some people in the area own homes but they want to 'upgrade' the property while remaining in the area. They have already been thinking about upsizing and now your home is being presented as a reason to take action.

Some people in the area are renting, but they want to buy in the area.

And lastly, some people know friends or family that like the neighbourhood and have discussed moving.

To speak with twenty decision-makers, plan to spend about two or three hours a day doing direct door-to-door marketing. In neighbourhoods with big yards expect to spend more time.

This works. Do it. It doesn't matter if you find it fun or not. I doubt anyone ever finds door-to-door marketing fun. But it does get results. You owe it to yourself as a private home-seller or you owe it to your clients as a real estate agent.

Chapter 25

CONTACT YOUR SPHERE OF INFLUENCE

Your sphere of influence (SOI) is everyone you know who is relevant in the potential purchase of your property or will know someone who is.

For home sellers, this list includes friends, co-workers, and other associates. For real estate agents, it includes previous home buyers, your investment buyers, mortgage brokers, bankers, inspectors, appraisers, lawyers, etc.

You want to let your SOI know about your real estate for sale. Just like with advertising to your local neighbourhood, this method brings surprisingly good results for the cost and effort involved.

Let your current buyers know about the property.

Share the details of the property with any of your current buyers and any current buyers for your brokerage. If you can do this right away buyers like to have an 'insider knowledge' of what is for sale right when it comes available. This gives them the edge to buy the property if they can buy a good property and beat other buyers to the punch.

This is a group of motivated buyers that is sitting right in your pocket – take advantage of it. Getting motivated buyers to your seller's property fast helps them sell fast and for more money. So don't be shy, tell them!

Contact your list of past buyers.

Past buyers are a great source of buyer leads for the property you have for sale.

If your past buyers had indicated they were interested in future purchases, and if the property matches something you know they are interested in, then contact those past buyers that fit this property.

Then contact your investment property buyers if this fits their portfolio.

This is the group that is least likely to buy the property for market value. Investment buyers are generally only looking for properties that are being sold at a discount.

That isn't what you want for your client.

But that doesn't mean you should ignore this group. You should still be contacting your investment property buyers because you still want to get as many people potentially bidding on the property as is possible.

Contact the real estate professionals you work with.

Do not overlook this. If you've done only three or four real estate transactions, you've already probably met about a dozen professionals connected with real estate. Home inspectors, appraisers, mortgage brokers, bankers, lawyers, contractors, etc. If you met three different professionals just from that list you already have eighteen people in your sphere of influence that you can leverage to benefit your client and get a better sale.

There is a massive leveraging power in dealing with other professionals – which is they also deal with many people. Those professionals also have a list of people in the real estate market.

This is something where most private sellers simply can't compete with real estate agents unless they are also in the real estate business somehow and also have those same connections. Having those connections means that the professionals in your list know 5 people in the real estate market. They also know 20 other professionals that are in real estate somehow and those 20 people each know 5 people in the market and 20 other professionals. Instead of contacting a dozen people, you've got a potential reach of hundreds with a single 'Just Listed' email. You can see how that is a force multiplier.

Take advantage of this and utilize your SOI.

Chapter 26

HOLD AN OPEN HOUSE

There are differing opinions on open houses for selling real estate – both with home sellers and real estate agents. But I am a firm believer in hosting an open house and have many examples of success through them. While it won't sell the house there and then all the time – then again, if anything sold a house there and then all the time that's all we'd ever do – it does frequently enough that it shouldn't be ignored and your home sale deserves every advantage you can give it.

So why host an open house?

It gives you a second round of local marketing.

Your first round of local marketing should be the 'Just Listed' cards that you delivered to the neighbourhood. But the thing in marketing is one touch doesn't usually work on its own. You typically need multiple touches to get the sale. An open house provides the reason for those multiple touches. You could just send another post-card. But if you're sending the same ad with the same message it eventually becomes white noise that the reader immediately ignores as nothing new. An open house, however, is new.

It brings people in the neighbourhood who were only slightly interested to see the property out of curiosity.

Some people hate this. They call them the 'looky-loos'. I'm more than happy to have the 'looky-loos' come check out the property. Why not? How does that hurt the home sale process? It doesn't at all.

It isn't rude for them to come to look even if they have no interest in buying. That's kind of the point of the open house. It's open because, for this one event, we don't have any pre-qualifications for people seeing the property. (Every other time we must have pre-qualifications for showing the house, but I will cover that in another chapter.)

I have been involved in more than one situation where a person in the neighbourhood was only mildly curious about a property from the ads, but then gave me a lead to the person that ultimately bought the property for my client. That would never have happened without an open house, and without welcoming the 'looky-loos'.

It gives agents the ability to preview your property for their clients.

Previewing property for clients is a pretty common event for real estate agents. Some clients want to see every property with their agent; some want their agent to do the legwork and disqualify any property that wouldn't meet their criteria once they see it in person.

The best means to give an agent to preview a property is the open house. It works best for you and them. It works for you because you don't have to schedule a showing for a real estate agent without a buyer present. Personally, I don't like doing that and my sellers don't like doing that. But there are situations where this is what is needed. An open house gives them the means to do so with as little intrusion on your life as is possible.

Some buyers prefer open houses.

People are busy, and homebuyers are no exception. Sometimes what a couple will do to save time and energy is tour the area that they are interested in and visit open houses unannounced. They often make an outing of this type of activity.

Some buyers also like open houses because they feel less intimidating or high pressure. After all, it is an open house. Some of these buyers shop exclusively with open houses because of that easy feeling.

If you aren't hosting an open house, then you're not available to this section of the home buyer market.

Open houses give buyers more time to view the property.

Most times a buyer is viewing a property with a scheduled viewing they are also viewing four other properties that same night. As a result, they sometimes only get 15 minutes per property to view it. They get in, then they get out.

An open house provides them with a more relaxed ability to spend more time viewing the details of the property and form a better opinion.

An open house has between a 1 in 20 and 1 in 30 chance of selling there and then.

This is the big reason why some people – both home sellers and real estate agents – prefer to skip the open house. Why bother with only a 1 in 20 chance of selling there and then?

I see this as saying we increase the chance of selling your property quickly and at a price you want by between 3% and 5% if we host an open house. Since we are increasing the chance of a sale, increasing exposure, and opening up your property to people that otherwise wouldn't even see it, I think hosting an open house is typically the way to go. The exceptions are if the property is not easily accessible or if the house is not well maintained or clean.

Chapter 27

MARKET THE OPEN HOUSE

You should hold your open house one or two weeks after the neighbourhood receives your 'Just Listed' cards. If you do it sooner than that then both impressions blur into just one event and you lose some marketing power. If you do it too late then people forget the just listed card and you're basically starting your impressions again; again losing the marketing power.

But holding the open house one or two weeks after they receive the first card is a good balance.

While mailing the Just Listed cards was acceptable, I find that door-to-door marketing is the absolute best for an open house.

Many people dislike going door-to-door. I understand that. It's intimidating to go up to someone's door and then solicit to them. It's probably one of the most intimidating sales methods that exists, and there's a reason why most people don't want to be door-to-door salespeople.

But it works. It works very well, especially in real estate, and especially with open houses.

Door-to-door marketing with an open house has a very personal touch. You aren't selling them anything. It's an invitation to come to visit the free open house. It's friendly and polite and gets great results.

There will be maybe one person in 20 who is unhappy that you knocked on their door. And about 1 in 100 who will be rude to you. If that happens just say thank you for your time, smile politely, and move on to the next door. You're not trying to bother anyone, so as soon as someone seems to be bothered, make it easy for them and move to the next one.

I don't know anyone who actually likes doing this (myself included). But do it anyway. It works.

Go door to door on a Wednesday or Thursday evening.

If you go on a Tuesday evening, then the event is too far away from when you talk to people and they forget about it. If you do it too close to the weekend, then people will already have plans.

So Wednesday and Thursday nights tend to get the best results. That should be the day you pick to go door to door.

Have a printed invitation.

Your invitation should include some photographs, the features and benefits, some advertising copy, the address, and the asking price. A single-page flyer works best. It also gives you a little more area to have more advertising copy than a postcard would.

Put up signs on the weekend of the open house.

Firstly, check with your municipal by-laws to see what restrictions there are on when and where you can put up open house signs. Then follow the by-laws. Some municipalities don't even allow these signs at all. If they don't, then don't put them up.

But if and when you are allowed to, put up signs on each corner that leads from the nearest major road to your open house. Like always, make these signs professional to project the right image of your home sale. A shoddy advertisement suggests a shoddy product. You don't want to project that. You want to project quality and value.

You Can Advertise the Open House on any free site you can find.

I don't recommend paying money for these advertisements, for reasons you'll read below in the 'Market Online' section. But using a free online classified is different. They rarely get results. But they are fast, easy, and free. Go ahead and advertise on them.

Chapter 28

ONLINE AND PRINT CLASSIFIEDS

Generally speaking, online and printed classifieds give an almost zero return. Most real estate agents don't bother advertising on even free classifieds. That should say something. It isn't because they are cheap or lazy. It's free and doesn't take much time. It's because they have learned through experience that there isn't must benefit to these ads.

I do sometimes put ads in the paper. This isn't because they have a good rate of success. In fact, I've never had a single sale from them. I've had some people call me about an ad. But never have I had a property sell from one. That's the same with most real estate agents and that's why most don't bother with them.

Putting up a real estate ad in the paper or online classifieds is done only because a seller might be nervous about the home selling process without one. I don't spend that money to sell the house; it's never done that. I do it to put my client at ease, and that can have enough value that I sometimes put in an ad.

If you are a private seller, though, I can't see how this can ever get any positive return. Most likely most callers will be real estate agents hoping to represent you.

Do have a real estate website or page.

The number one online marketing tool is undoubtedly a real estate page that has a direct feed from the MLS$^{®}$. This has been a fantastic source of property sales and this should be number one in your marketing inventory.

Use re-targeted ads.

Remember that most sales don't happen with just one impression. Typically, you need multiple impressions to get the sale.

There's a way to leverage the real estate page that is linked to the MLS$^{®}$ to be even more effective through using re-targeting ads.

Set up a 'tag' on the property page. This tag will be remembered by the viewers computer and Google.

Then you set up an advertisement of the property on Google Networks. Once this is done, any person who viewed the property page will re-see the ad for the property many times as they surf the net – even on totally different pages.

Any website which uses Google as an advertiser – and that's most websites – will have the potential to show that person the ad for the property multiple times. Anyone who had enough interest to see the property online in the first place will now see that ad many times over the span of a few days or weeks.

That's how you keep the property in the front of the mind of your potential buyer. Make sure to set your re-target parameters so that the customers aren't spammed. If they see it too much you'll have the opposite effect and just turn them off.

Chapter 29

ACTIVE MARKETING SUMMARY

That was a lot of information, so I'm going to write a summary of what to do with active, direct marketing and in what order.

1. List the property on the MLS$^{\circledR}$.

2. Set up a listing page on the internet that gets lots of traffic and that you can control the 'cookies' for retargeting ads.

3. Contact past buyers in your Sphere of Influence(SOI). Tell your current buyers looking for a property to buy about the property. Contact your past buyers and investment property buyers. Give them a "head's up" to come to see the property first.

4. Contact the professionals in your SOI.

5. Send out 'Just Listed' postcards. Either by direct mail or door to door. Mail is fine if you go door to door afterwards.

6. Make online and print classified ads if your client would feel more comfortable with that. But otherwise skip this, it has a nearly zero return on investment.

7. Just after the postcards are delivered, go door to door with a flyer this time of your property for sale. Do this for two hours a day for five days a week until the house is sold. No need to knock on the same doors of people you spoke to already. But do repeat knocking on doors that didn't answer previously. Start close to the property and move outwards each day. The farther you go from the subject property the less effective this will be.

8. Two weeks after the 'Just Listed' postcards are delivered, schedule an open house. Go door to door with invitations to the open house on either the Wednesday or Thursday before the open – or both!

9. Host the open house.

Chapter 30

SHOWING THE PROPERTY

Now that you've effectively marketed the property, you need to show it to potential buyers. This chapter will go over some tips and tricks to have the property show its best.

Be available to show the property with little to no notice.

Now that you're in selling mode, you have to be ready to show the property with as little notice as possible – because you will likely get many requests with little notice.

You should consider 10 am to 8 pm to be showing hours – whether you have a showing booked or not. The name of the game now is to have as many potential buyers view the property as quickly as possible.

Bookings are almost always done in a range covering one hour. Most real estate agents will arrange many viewings at a time for their clients. They do this because it is efficient and it gives their clients more samples of housing for them to compare and make an

educated decision on the options available to them. Since they are
going from property to property, and since they don't know how
long they will be at each property, they tend to schedule a range
of one hour to cover the schedule. In reality, most viewings are
between ten and twenty minutes long. The extra time is to cushion
the unknown exact time of when they will be leaving the last
property and heading to yours.

Keep the house spotless at all times.

Since you should be ready to have showings with little to no
notice, you won't have time to declutter and clean up the place. You
have to maintain that high level of cleanliness always.

That also means before you go to work in the morning, you have
to make sure the property is in show-ready condition. This way if
you get a request while you are at work you can still show it and
not lose that potential sale.

Having unavailable hours because the property isn't clean and
tidy means fewer viewings, fewer parties willing to put in an offer,
and likely a lower selling price.

Set the temperature to room temperature for the whole day.

Most thermostats are set to be room temperature only during the
hours you are there. This makes sense to save costs when you don't
need the heat. But you also don't want your customers feeling the
property is too cold or too hot. Have it set to room temperature
from 10 am to 8 pm while you are selling.

Make the table as if you were expecting a small dinner party with wine.

If there is one cheap, easy, and effective way to have the property
before you show it, it's this.

Depending on the size of your dinner table, set between four and
six places on it. Have a placemat; dinner plate; knives, forks, and
spoons; unlit candles; flowers; and wine glasses. It is elegant and
welcoming to viewers, and costs next to nothing.

Sellers should not be there when the property is shown.

Sellers sometimes want to be at the house when it is being shown. They often think that they can talk about all the good things about the property and help sell it.

It is the exact opposite. It hurts the sale. Don't be there.

There's a rule in real estate to not do anything that makes the property feel crowded and small. Having too many people in a room – especially when they are strangers and must have a large personal space before feeling uncomfortable – makes the property feel smaller than it really is.

It doesn't matter how smooth you are, if the seller is following the potential buyers around it makes them seem clingy and desperate for a sale. And desperation never equates to giving the highest and best offer.

It makes the vast majority of buyers uncomfortable when the seller is present. The comments I've had when leaving a showing with clients when the sellers are there are almost always how they felt stressed and on edge for that showing. You don't want your customers feeling stressed when they are viewing your product. You want them to feel at ease, comfortable, and relaxed. Otherwise, they will associate your property with stress, and the other properties with comfort. That's not what you want.

Do not be there when showing.

Now, of course, this tip is not available to sellers who are selling the home themselves. It is only possible when a seller is working with real estate agents.

If you're selling yourself, you don't really have a choice but to skip this tip. But it will likely have a negative effect on the final sale price.

Take out the garbage.

It will help the property smell fresh and garbage is unsightly.

Have some fresh baked cookies out for guests to take.

Most people know this trick, and most viewers will know what you're trying to do when you have baking. That can reduce the effectiveness if people think you're trying to manipulate their emotions.

But if you bake cookies and leave a note with the baking inviting your guests to have some cookies, they take it as being generous. That gives an excuse for the baking smell. You weren't trying to make the house seem homey with smells. You were giving them a gift, and the good smell was just a product of that.

This is a tough one to get right since you also need to have the place looking spotless. So how do you do that and bake at the same time? Have some pre-made cookie dough – home-made or store-bought – ready and put them on a baking sheet to bake to finish just before you leave.

DO NOT LEAVE BEFORE YOU TAKE THEM OUT AND TURN OFF THE OVEN.

Then put them in a nice basket with a note for guests to help themselves.

This step isn't a must. You can sell a property perfectly well without this. But it is a nice touch that helps your property stand out from the rest.

Put away all cash and valuables.

I have personally never been involved in a situation where there was even a claim of theft – but it's bound to be a risk. Confidential papers, expensive jewelry and clothing, and all other valuables should be out of view and locked up.

Turn on all the lights in the house.

We've already changed all the lights to help the property show as bright and spacious. Now's the time to use them.

Go through the property and turn on all the lights in the entire property. Dark spaces make people tighten up and look with caution what they are approaching. You don't want any anxiety in your customers. They shouldn't have to turn on a single light or see a speck of darkness because the lights should all be on already.

Most real estate agents will leave the property as they found it. So if you had lights on, they'll leave lights on. If you had them off, they'll turn them off. That's good because it means most agents won't turn off the lights if there's another showing coming after them.

Put away all pets.

A good solution is to not have pets on the premises during a showing. You would do best if you removed all evidence that there ever were pets on the property. But if that isn't possible, the next best solution is to have them put where they can't get out, don't interfere with the showing (so putting them in a room isn't a solution as buyers will want to view that room), and don't cause any odours or noise.

This is how professionals want to show a home. Do what the professionals do and you'll have more likelihood of success.

Some sellers are unable to remove pets or have them where they can't get out. That happens. If it does, you will likely still be able to sell the property. Just be aware that it's a negative factor towards selling it for top market value. Also, there have been instances where real estate agents and homebuyers have been attacked by animals. Home sellers have a duty to ensure that people they invite into the property to view it for a potential purchase are not endangered by their animals. Again, it is best to not have them on the premises.

Chapter 31

Property Showing and Open House Safety

In most situations, real estate transactions are safe.

But there have been situations where people have been injured or killed doing what they expected to be a simple showing of a property. Murder, sexual assault, being tied up, robbery, and other violence are risks that, while uncommon, have been suffered by both real estate agents and private sellers.

This chapter is to discuss some strategies to minimize that risk.

The most common event for such an assault is during a home showing or during an open house. There are many reasons why these two events hold a particular risk.

Firstly, it involves being in a place that is about as private as a place can be. It isn't in the public view. There are usually no staff of businesses with a direct view. The house is designed for privacy. This means that there are no witnesses against a person who wants to commit a crime.

Secondly, it often involves strangers. When you are selling a property most of the time you don't know the people that are going to be interested in the home. Not knowing who you will be meeting increases the risk.

So how do we better protect ourselves?

Work in teams.

There is strength in numbers with safety, and you should not be doing this alone. Many of the safety tips revolve around other people supporting you.

If you are a real estate professional, that team is your brokerage.

Private sellers should use family and friends. Real estate agents can use family or friends as your team as well. But have them in place and ready to help you with security. That doesn't always mean they have to be there. In some situations, it just means they have a phone with them and are aware that you might need to call them.

Show the house with a team.

If you are selling privately especially, do not show the property alone to someone you don't know. Have a team member with you.

If you are doing a first-time showing with a new customer, arrange for a team member to join you in showing the property. After you know your client (below), you have more safety to show alone.

Inform team members of a meeting.

Tell your team who you are meeting and when; the customer's name(s) and phone number(s); where you are going; when you expect to be back; and schedule a check-up call with your team to make sure you are ok.

Call your team member while you are with the customer.

While your customer is with you, call your team on the phone and let them know where you will be and tell them you will be with the customer by name.

Know Your Customer/Client (KYC).

If there is a single, number one rule to follow it is this. Know your customer.

Here are some ways to know your customer before you are alone with them in a property.

Show the house by appointment or open house only.

If someone shows up at the house hoping for a viewing, you should collect their information, especially their phone number, and tell them you can't show it now but you or your real estate agent will call them to set up an appointment.

If you hired a real estate agent, pass on the information to them.

If you are selling privately, then contact the prospect a short while later by the phone number they gave you.

Keep between the customer and the exit.

As much as you can, try not to let your customer get between you and the exit. This is to keep a path of escape available to you.

Be ready to run.

Choose flight over fight. You don't want to resist any violence, you want to get away from it.

Keep your cell phone fully charged and in your hand.

It's there to call for help, but also it can be used as an improvised weapon if you need to protect yourself with a strike before you run.

Wear shoes that can run.

Don't choose shoes that will inhibit your ability to run.

Take a self-defence class.

You don't want to fight, but knowing how to fight and being practiced at it could mean the ability to get out of grasp and then running.

Have a distress code.

This is an old trick in banking and other professions that risk robbery. Have your team member call and ask to know where a file is. Have a code for the answer. One code means you're safe, the other means you are not safe. You don't want it to be obvious which one means what.

Practice the codes because you don't want to mess this up if you need it.

If the distress code is given, the team member should immediately contact the police with the information you provided them about where you are, with who, and the license plate.

Schedule showings and open houses during the daylight hours.

This is better for the sales process anyway. But it is also better for safety.

Have the first meeting at an office or in public.

This is a good first step to know who is about to be in your home with you. If you have a real estate office, try to meet there. If you can't arrange that, then arrange to meet in a public area.

For real estate agents, this is the perfect time to have them sign either an agency acknowledgement (which is not a contract), or to have them sign a buyer brokerage agreement (which is a contract). When doing this, ask to see the ID of the person. You need to verify the identity of anyone signing these documents, anyway. So this makes a perfect reason to check ID.

Verify that the ID meets all the counter-forgery methods that the ID uses. Verify that the person in front of you resembles the photograph. Then let the potential client watch you write down their names and ID numbers on either the agency acknowledgement or the contract. You should have that information for either of those anyway, so doing so now kills two birds with one stone. You are getting your paperwork done and taking an important KYC step.

Another option is to have them meet with another professional who also must check their ID – such as a mortgage professional. You will want a copy of a pre-approval if this is the means you want to use to check ID, and you'll want to know the habits of the mortgage professional – such as not issuing pre-approvals remotely.

Write down the license plate number of the vehicle they came in.

If you are feeling uneasy, you can let the customer see you do this. If you don't feel uneasy, do it privately. But do it in both cases.

If you are showing them that you are recording their plate numbers, let them know this is a standard safety precaution and that you cannot proceed without this.

Then text that plate number to a member of your team.

A criminal will now think that the police will quickly have the means to track them if they commit a crime.

Set up an open house for safety.

Always put away any valuables and important documents before an open house.

Also, make the house interior as visible as possible. Open the curtains and turn on all the lights.

Have an excuse ready for why you need to go.

Whether you need to take a call, or make a call, or schedule an appointment, it doesn't matter. But have an excuse ready for why you need to go and be alone. Use this excuse if you ever feel uncomfortable.

Have three team members at your open house.

For real estate agents, have the hosting agent and a helping agent. Also, have a mortgage professional on site.

Do a thorough search of the property after the open house.

In teams, go through the house and check all the places that someone can hide after the open house. It's easy to lose track of who comes in and goes out during a busy open house. You want to make sure no people are hiding.

Trust your spidey-sense.

Trust your instincts and any sense of concern or fear. If you feel fear or trepidation then assume it is there for a reason, even if you can't grasp where the feeling is coming from.

Always act as if your instinct is always right – even if it isn't. It's better for you to make a mistake and be cautious than to ignore your instincts and end up hurt.

Crimes committed against homeowners and real estate agents are not common – but they do happen. They also happen with enough regularity that everyone should be following these security measures when selling real estate.

Even these do not guarantee that a person is safe, but they do increase the likelihood of it. These are industry standards for a reason – follow them.

Chapter 32

When to Lower the Asking Price

This is the last thing we want to do.

If you are doing all the right steps as listed in this book towards pricing and marketing the property, this should happen under one and only one situation: the entire real estate market is dropping.

If that happens then there isn't much choice but to drop the price according to the market. Otherwise, even if the property was originally well priced, it is now over-priced and will suffer the same consequences as any other over-priced property.

If you are actively marketing the property as described in this book, and the market isn't dropping, but you still don't have a sale that can only mean one thing. You over-priced it from the beginning. You need to correct this.

How long should you wait before you lower the price?

You should be monitoring the market every day for changes. If market drop patterns are happening, review your marketing plan and see if you should be pre-emptively adjusting your price.

But if that isn't happening, and if you priced it right from the start, there's no need to be lowering the price after only a few days or even a few weeks.

If did not overprice and if the market isn't obviously dropping, you should wait until you are about 2/3 the way to the average days on market or 80 days, whichever is less. If the average days on market is currently 60 days, and if you don't have an accepted offer by day 40, then it's time to lower the price. Otherwise, you're heading towards having both an over-priced and a stale property. Either one of those will hurt your sale – both together hurts it even more.

However, if the market is obviously dropping or if you ignored the advice on pricing properly and decided to over-price the house, then you should be considering a price drop sooner than later. You should do it immediately. It isn't helping you to keep the price high. It's hurting you. It makes it less likely to make the most money possible, not more.

If you lower the price, make it a big drop.

I know this isn't what any home seller wants to hear. But it's the truth. There is one thing worse than lowering the price: lowering it over and over again.

If you lower the price by a small amount, it isn't news. It isn't exciting. It isn't a deal. It's nothing special. If you read an advertisement with big bold letters that said 'PRICE REDUCED!' and then you found out they lowered just $1000.00 from the $399,000.00 asking price, what would you think? Most likely, 'who cares?' That's what buyers will think if you drop it a small amount as well.

If you aren't getting offers, your property likely isn't just a few points over-priced. So dropping it by a few points isn't going to fix the problem. All this will do is put you in the same boat and you will have to lower the price again – which is even worse for reasons I'll explain shortly.

No, you want a big drop. You want at least a 3% drop – maybe even more. That's big.

Firstly, do another market analysis. Find out what the sales price should be. If you went over that amount before, you absolutely cannot do so again if you want the best sale. You have to price it right this time. And you can't price it above market value at all. Not even that 1% we discussed earlier for the negotiating room.

So it doesn't matter if it's a 3% drop, a 6% drop, or even a 12% drop if it means the price is 3%, 6%, or 12% over market value. If it is priced 12% above market value, drop it by that entire 12%. Why would it be so much higher than market value, though? That's a mistake to over-price it so much.

Follow all the pricing strategies in setting the new price.

Go back to the section on pricing to see all the techniques used and reapply them to the new price.

The more often you lower the price, the worse the offers you get are likely to be.

You are far, far better off dropping the price by 6% than you are dropping it by 2% three times.

If you were buying a house and you saw that the seller is in a pattern of lowering the prices, what would you think? Most buyers think 'They won't mind lowering it again.'

If you keep lowering prices, then they'll think it's a bad deal at whatever current price you have, and they will offer even less. If you have a pattern of dropping the price by 2%, then the buyers will likely set their target price at no more than 2% less than whatever price it is now. Their initial offer will therefore be even lower than that.

That is not what you want buyers to be thinking. You want them to be thinking this is a hot property and they have got to jump on it.

You might have to accept that you won't get the best price you could have if you are lowering prices.

If a property could have been sold for $400,000 but was over-priced at $416,000 and now needs to be dropped, these are the circumstances that lead to a property selling for less than it could have.

It is becoming stale. The sellers have a history of dropping prices. It doesn't seem like there're many people, if anyone, interested in competing with the buyer to get the deal.

A property that could have otherwise gone for $400,000 might well sell for a few percentage points less if you overpriced it. Now you might only be able to get $390-$395k in the final sales price.

All this comes down to pricing it right the first time.

This is why pricing it right the first time and then getting out of the gate with a fast, exciting marketing campaign is so important. It's to avoid ever being in the situation where you have to lower prices.

If you're pricing and marketing the property well, this shouldn't be an issue. But if it becomes an issue, fix it quickly and decisively.

Chapter 33

WHEN TO SELL YOURSELF & WHEN TO HIRE A REAL ESTATE AGENT

There is a time and place for choosing to sell real estate by yourself, and there's a time and place when you should choose a real estate agent to sell your property. This chapter will go over a few considerations on which choice is best for a home seller based on their own experience and situation.

It is entirely possible for a for sale by owner to have similar results as a real estate agent. A real estate agent does not have any magical ability, and all the things that a real estate agent can do to sell a house a private seller can also do.

But here's the other side of that. Real estate agents are far more experienced than private sellers. Most homeowners stay in their homes for 7 to 10 years or even more. Even a real estate agent that only sells one house a month has 84 times as much experience as that.

Realtors will be selling property full-time. Most homeowners cannot dedicate the same amount of time to selling a property as a professional can.

And real estate agents are not shy about acting like salespeople. They are salespeople. That's their job. If you want to get the best results in sales, you have to use the sales methods.

But those sales methods aren't any secret or mystery. They are right here in this book. If you do all the things in this book then you are doing all the same steps that the best real estate agents would do. If you don't do all the same steps that the best salespeople do, then you shouldn't expect to get as good results as the best salespeople.

So if you are wondering which is the best option for you, here are some points to consider.

Reasons to consider selling yourself.

You already have a buyer in place.

This is the most obvious reason to sell by yourself. It also accounts for nearly half of for sale by owner successes. You do want to make sure this is a viable buyer, of course.

You might still want to engage a Realtor to get a 'mere posting' in this situation, as having a property on the MLS$^{\circledR}$ makes the financing easier for the buyer and the bank. Mere listings should not have the same cost, and you should be able to get that for a fixed fee of a few hundred dollars.

You are not busy in life or work.

If you are already finding that you are busy in your life or your work then there isn't much point in adding to that stress by putting another task on your plate. And this is a big task that likely involves one of your most expensive assets.

If you are already busy, selling your property yourself will make your existing tasks even more difficult to accomplish. That's pretty straightforward. Are you more or less likely to succeed with your work if you take time away from it to sell your house? Obviously, you are less likely. The same is true for your personal life.

Additionally, if you are already busy, that means that the chances of you being able to give the home sale the attention it deserves is not likely.

If you are busy, you should hire a real estate agent to sell the property.

If you are not busy in your work life or personal life, however, then you should have the ability to devote the appropriate attention

You can give access to show the property from 10 am to 8 pm.

If you are not able to give access to potential buyers every day within this timeframe with only one to two hours' notice, then you are going to miss out on potential buyers. Having fewer potential buyers means less competition to buy your property, and that usually means a lower price.

You are willing to pay for the costs upfront.

Most, but not all, real estate agents will arrange a situation where they take all the upfront financial risk themselves. They will pay for the MLS® listing, the professional photographer, an accurate floor plan, the 3D virtual home tour, signage, postcards, etc, themselves.

These can all easily add up to more than $1000.00 in the first week.

If the Realtor doesn't sell the property, then that's their loss.

Just like the Realtor, the private seller also needs to have all those done in the first week if they want a good marketing plan. If they fail to sell then they are out of the upfront costs, the time lost, and having a now stale property.

It isn't in your personality to ever think of any offer as 'insulting.'

This is business. There's nothing personal in any offer. But most home sellers still feel that low offers are a personal insult to them or to their home. This is very common. But you should think twice about selling your property yourself if you could imagine yourself ever feeling insulted for any offer. If you do, there's a strong chance emotions could pop up in the sale or negotiation stages that sabotage your sale. Having a real estate agent act as a buffer and giving unemotional advice is likely in your best interest in this case.

You are a 'people person.'

Real estate is very much a person-to-person, face-to-face industry. It always has been, and the internet hasn't changed that in the slightest.

You will have to engage with people directly and show them the property. How the people relate to you will affect their purchase decision-making process. If you and others describe you as a 'people person' then selling yourself could be a viable option for you.

You are a top salesperson.

Is your profession sales? Are you consistently one of the top achievers in sales in your job? Do your co-workers say you could sell sand in the desert? Since this is such a significant asset, it seems reasonable to want someone who can sell sand in a desert in charge of selling your property. If this describes you then that is a point for selling yourself.

You already have experience selling houses.

The more experienced you are, the better you will be able to succeed in selling the house. Selling one house one time does not make a person experienced. But after three or four sales your experience is likely building to say the least.

You understand this is going to take hard work.

If anyone is telling you it is easy to be a top salesperson, that person isn't being that honest. If it were easy and everyone could do it, there wouldn't be any such thing as a top salesperson. It isn't easy. It takes hard, constant work. If you're ready to put in that work, then selling yourself is a viable option for you.

You are able and willing to actively market your property.

Just putting up signs, listing it on the MLS$^{\circledR}$, and putting up online or print ads is not active marketing. To get the top market value you need to have all those and still do direct marketing to both potential buyers and spheres of influence.

You are willing to solicit to your sphere of influence.

You are willing to host an open house.

You are willing to go door-knocking to promote the property.

You are willing and able to contact twenty decision-making prospects per day in person or on the phone.

You have a sphere of influence already established.

If you have twelve people or more that know you and like you, and their business deals with people who are buying real estate, then you have a significant advantage that you should leverage. Reach out to this group to let them know about your property for sale.

You are willing to share the savings with the buyer.

When someone is looking to buy a used car they have two choices: buy from a used dealership or buy from a private seller. When they choose to go to a private seller, they tend to want to pay a lower price compared to going to a dealership. Why would a buyer go from house to house looking at cars if they could go to a dealership and have all the options right there if the cars are selling for the same price? The reason buyers are willing to go through that effort of a private sale is only because they expect to pay a lower price for the same product. Otherwise, they wouldn't do it.

The same is true for home buyers as soon as they see that a property is being sold for sale by owner. They know that the seller won't be paying a commission, so they expect to pay a lower price and get a good deal themselves as well, and they can feel insulted if that doesn't happen.

If all of these describe you, you are likely suited to sell the property alone. If you found yourself doubting three or more of these as applying to your situation, then you should consider it best to hire a real estate agent to get your house sold.

Reasons to consider hiring a real estate agent.

If three or more of the recommendations above do not apply to you then you probably shouldn't be selling the property on your own. Additionally, here are a few other situations where it makes sense to hire a real estate agent.

You don't want to pay until after a successful deal is done.

When selling privately, all the upfront costs are paid by you. If the house doesn't sell, you're out the $1000.00 it costs for the MLS$^{®}$ listing, signage, photographer, floor plan, 3D virtual tour, 'Just Listed' postcards, and any other marketing costs. If the house doesn't sell, you spent all that money with nothing to show for it.

If you hire a real estate agent they take that risk themselves. Now it's up to them to get the property sold or not only have they spent months working for no money, they also take a financial loss.

If you'd rather pay only for performance, then a real estate agent with a commission paid only after the house is sold and the money is sent to your lawyer is the way to go.

You want someone who is dedicated to making the sale happen.

A real estate agent on a commission makes no money at all if the sale doesn't happen. That gives them a significant incentive to get the job done. Half done for them means zero income.

Who would be more committed to making the sale than someone who risks a great deal of work with potentially no income unless they succeed?

You want a professional to do all the paperwork.

If you are concerned about the paperwork and legal contracts then it is a good idea to get someone to do it for you. A lawyer can also fulfill this role. So you can choose to hire a real estate agent or choose a lawyer for this one.

This isn't a trivial aspect. Many issues can go wrong with a real estate contract that isn't properly done.

The sale could be invalid. Simple errors in the contract can make a sale invalid; such as incorrect dates or legal descriptions, missing the expiry deadline of the contract, lack of consideration, unlawful consideration or subject matter, or legal capacity of the signors. If you don't know what those mean immediately, then you should hire a professional to manage the contract. The last thing you want after working to prepare, market, then sell the property is for the contract to not be worth the paper it's printed on. Or worse.

You could be sued. You want the contract to be designed to protect your interests. If the contract isn't designed so, and if you then had little choice but to breach it to protect yourself, you then might line yourself up for a lawsuit. You don't want to spend the money on a lawyer, months in court, and potentially a large settlement. Getting it right is important. If you are unsure that you have the training and experience to write a proper contract, hire a professional lawyer or real estate agent.

The steps needed are:

1 – Write the contract

2 – Deliver the contract to the other party before the contract expires.

3 – Get the contract back from the other party before it expires. It will be either accepted, rejected, or it will be a counter-offer. If it is rejected, you can attempt to re-engage with a new offer – go to step 1. If it keeps being rejected it might be best to find a new buyer. If it is a counter-offer go to step 4. If it is accepted go to step 6.

4 – Review the counter-offer. Either accept the counter or choose to give a counter-offer of your own. If you choose to counter the offer go to step 5. If you accept the counter go to step 6.

5 – Write the counter-offer. Change the expiry of the agreement. Go back to step 2.

6 – Finalize the contract and deliver copies to all parties.

The cost for a lawyer could easily be between $250 and $350 an hour in 2021 for each step your deal ends up needing. But there will be different costs in different markets. A real estate agent will usually have that included in their commission once the house is sold.

You want a good deal of experience.

Unless they are selling a dozen properties a year, a private seller can never have the same level of experience that a good real estate agent has. There is no way that they will have encountered all the same problems – and learned the solutions to fix those problems – that come up in real estate transactions unless they have sold dozens of homes.

You want to get professional step-by-step advice without a large hourly fee.

A Realtor on a commission agreement is available to advise you on every step of the home sale process. Since they are on commission, that advice doesn't cost you anything extra.

You want a professional marketing plan.

You don't need a real estate agent for this. You have a professional marketing plan in your hands right now. If you can follow this step by step, then you're good to go on marketing. If you can't follow this step by step for whatever reason, then it is best to hire a real estate agent that will.

You don't want to show the house yourself.

I strongly recommend not being there for home showings. Buyers don't usually tell the home seller they prefer that the seller not be there because they are being polite. But once they are on the driveway heading to the cars, they consistently tell real estate agents how uncomfortable that makes them feel. You want them to feel at home in the property to get them thinking about living there, and then buying it. You don't want them feeling uncomfortable. They will be thinking of the property as less of a potential home if they are uncomfortable.

If you are doing for-sale-by-owner, there is really no way to avoid this. You need to be escorting them through the property. But this is a negative to selling on your own and one for private sellers to be aware of.

You aren't always available to show the house from 10 am to 8 pm.

If you are forced by your circumstances to limit your business hours, you could easily be missing out on buyers that would be ready to buy it. Having limited hours is a big hindrance to selling for the top price.

Real estate agents have a huge advantage here. They set up a lockbox that can only be accessed by other real estate agents. So even if you aren't able to give access to the property because you are at work or the gym, then the property can still be accessed and the property will still be shown.

You want to have up-to-date market reviews.

The real estate market changes daily. So having a review of the overall market conditions daily gives the seller a greater ability to make an educated decision during the sales process.

Real estate agents have access to the daily hot sheets and can inform you of any pertinent changes.

You want someone else to do the work.

If your life is busy and you would rather be doing something other than real estate sales, then hiring a Realtor makes sense.

You want someone with Errors and Omissions Insurance.

In addition to having the experience that will reduce the likelihood of a lawsuit, a real estate agent must have Errors and Omissions (E&O) Insurance to protect against lawsuits due to mistakes. A private seller simply doesn't have access to this.

You understand that even though Realtors have a large commission, homes sold with them tend to sell for a higher value than those sold privately.

It's a real paradox.

Real estate agent commissions can indeed be very large.

But it is also true that statistics show the average price of a property sold using a real estate agent is higher than the average price of a property sold privately. Additionally, that difference in average prices is greater than 7%.

That means that the average net dollars earned by a property sold with a real estate agent are greater than the average net dollars earned by a private seller.

According to these statistics, the average home seller has more money in their pocket from the property sale when they hire a Realtor. That is why many real estate agents say they don't cost money, they make money.

Real estate agents are pros at generating interest in the property and then converting that interest to an enforceable sales contract. Whereas many for sale by owners find themselves struggling to find interested buyers and close the deal.

In 2020, for sale by owners accounted for only 9% of successful home sales. We also know that roughly half of all private sales were 'closely held' – meaning they were transactions between two parties that had already agreed to the sale (which is one of the reasons to consider FSBO).

This data implies that only around 4.5% of home sales are from a private seller to a person that wasn't already in place to buy the property.

This is why despite the internet providing all the same ability as the MLS® to have instant access to anyone, anywhere in the world, the majority of property sales are still done using real estate agents.

That also explains why the percentage of homes sold by a Realtor has not been decreasing. It has been increasing. The peak of homes sold privately was 14% in 2004. It's now 9%. If good real estate agents didn't provide good value for their cost, they would have been losing market share consistently. But we see the opposite has been happening.

But these are all dry statistics. Let's see some real-world examples. I have three stories that deserve to be shared about this topic.

I started my real estate career with a for sale by owner website.

The idea of saving money makes sense and real estate commissions can get pretty big. I thought it would make great sense to go for-sale-by-owner. That's why I got my license – to start a for-sale-by-owner website that utilizes the MLS®.

I built a website called MyFlatFee.ca. I was very proud of it. It was a place for home sellers to sell privately, but I used the MLS® as well. This gave my clients a great combination of being able to sell on their own with no commission percentage paid, and also getting maximal exposure with the MLS®. It also signalled to real estate agents that they were welcome to bring their buyers there.

I got my very first listing in only a week. Most new real estate agents go months before getting a listing, if not longer. I got my second listing just a few days after that. Both of these were from people I had never met before, but they found my marketing. Getting listings with a FSBO website was easy.

I simply priced my services under the other for sale by owner sites in the market. ComFree, the largest local for sale by owner website, had a price of something like $600 or so at the time. I put my price at $495 and that included the MLS$^{®}$ fee. At the time ComFree didn't have an option to also use the MLS$^{®}$. So I was offering more for less. Getting people to sign up was simple.

The money was great. If I got three listings a week I would make $1500 a week for only about four or five hours of work. No walking door to door. It was just internet ads and a website. The only thing I had to do was be there to sign people up and take photographs. I was a professional photographer so I was able to do that myself without hiring out.

But I noticed something. While I was getting listings without much effort, I noticed that they weren't selling as well as I expected.

One might think that shouldn't make a difference to me since I already got paid. But I didn't want to make money selling something that wasn't really helping people.

It wasn't because the website was lacking anything. Since every property I listed also had an MLS$^{®}$ listing that meant those properties were shown on literally hundreds of websites. There was tonnes of exposure. But it was all passive. I didn't know that yet, though.

So I attended a week-long real estate selling workshop to see what else I could do to help my clients' listings sell. That was where I learned the difference between passive and active real estate marketing.

I decided to do an A/B test. I started a regular real estate website with me taking a commission. This wasn't going to be a FSBO structure. This was full-service real estate using active marketing techniques. I got far fewer listings, of course – but more sold houses. In fact, I have only ever failed to sell one property since I started using the strategies in this book.

That convinced me. It was much harder work to do the active selling but it had results.

I decided to phase out the MyFlatFee.ca website. But I couldn't take it down right away as all my packages included 12 months on the MLS$^{®}$ and on my website. I had to honour those contracts so I had to keep that website up for another year. But I didn't want to do that business model anymore. I tripled the prices so I wouldn't get any new clients on it. That worked. The calls stopped immediately.

Since then, I have been dedicated to the active selling approach. I advise all real estate agents to do the same, and for private sellers to do so as well.

I was involved with a duplex sale where one half sold FSBO and the other half with a full-service real estate agent managing the sale.

I got a call from a young couple that was looking to buy a duplex. They had already found the home and had already seen it. It was being sold privately. But they still wanted me to represent them for the purchase. They had met me when they came to an open house I was hosting for another property, and they liked how I was straightforward with them.

I told them I was happy to represent them here, but I wanted to let them know that they don't require a real estate agent in this situation. They can purchase this property on their own without a Realtor. They told me they knew that, but they wanted me to represent them for guidance and protection against mistakes. I told them that is fine, but if they do sign a contract with me, then they must pay me a commission with the purchase – but that we can also work that into the contract so it is paid from the proceeds of the property sale so they don't need any cash out of pocket. They liked that, so we signed a buyer-brokerage agreement.

They had found a duplex from a FSBO website that also used the MLS®. It was asking $260,000.00. It was a very nice property that was well looked after and showed very well.

My clients told me they were willing to pay up to $250,000.00. That amount was slightly over what I thought the property was worth, but only by a few points. Also, it's still good to know what a client's comfort level is.

Since this was a private sale and since it had been on the market longer than the average 60 days on market(it was stale), I was not expecting much competition for the purchase, so I recommended that we start aggressively with a much lower offer. I recommended we open with $220,000 and that my commission is paid from that.

My clients wanted me to preview the property to give my opinion if there was an obvious reason why they shouldn't buy the property. We didn't want the seller to know that this offer would be coming from the same people that saw the property. It is better for us if they think that opportunity is dead. So I informed the seller I was coming to preview the property alone.

Since we are going so low, I recommended that my clients fill out an offer to purchase with that amount and have it signed and ready for acceptance. If you're going to go low, you want to show that you're serious and make it super easy for the seller to just sign. That makes it more likely for them to just accept the low-ball offer, or to make a counter-offer that isn't much higher. My clients' instructions to me were to give the offer unless I saw an obvious reason not to.

I didn't see any reason obvious to me not to. So after previewing the property I handed the seller the signed offer to purchase. He was stunned and didn't expect that. It was a very low-ball offer. But it was right there in his hand. That makes an impact.

The seller did not accept that offer of $220,000, but after a few rounds of negotiation we reached an agreed price of $230,000 – a full $30,000 less than asking, and $20,000 less than my clients were ready and willing to pay (of course, I didn't tell the sellers that information).

It was a great win. My clients were thrilled. If they had bought that property alone then they would have paid $20,000 more. It is a great feeling when you can so obviously show how you saved your clients enough money to pay for a car or a few years of university for their kids.

But then something interesting happened.

Just one week after this deal was completed, the other half of the duplex was also put up for sale by another owner who hired a real estate agent.

This is the other half of the exact same property, and happening within weeks of each other. Both halves were well maintained and both showed well. You can't get a better comparison than that.

Those sellers listed their half of the same duplex for $250,000.00. Unlike the private sale, this property did not last over two months without a sale. It sold in less than two weeks for $245,000.00.

I don't know what the commission paid was but if it was a 7/3 commission arrangement it would come to $11,350.00 plus $567.50 GST for a total of $11,917.50. With that commission structure, those sellers would have netted $233,082.50. The FSBO sellers didn't even gross that much. Going for-sale-by-owner did not mean more money for these private sellers.

The people who listed their half of the property privately took more than four times as long to get the property sold. They had less money in their pocket at the end of the day even considering the higher commission the other family likely paid to their real estate agent. And they did all the work themselves.

That's because they didn't follow a plan like you are getting in this book.

They overpriced the property. The difference in the asking prices was only $10,000, which is only 4%. But being overpriced by only 4% can make the difference between a house that is sold for the top market value, and a house that is sold for much less.

They didn't actively market the property. They had an MLS[®] listing, lawn sign, and multiple internet ads. They relied on passive marketing.

They were also less skilled in negotiation than they would like to admit. But then again, most people are. If someone doesn't negotiate for large deals daily, there's no way they will have the same experience in negotiation as someone who does. I used some negotiation tactics to influence them to accept a lower price, and those tactics worked.

The sellers on the other side of the duplex obviously did it right, because it sold fast and at the top market value.

There's one last interesting story, but this time it doesn't involve me.

The founder of a successful FSBO website had better success with a Realtor[®].

In New York, there was a man named Colby Sambrotto. He was one of the founders of a website for private sellers called ForSaleByOwner.com. The website provided a way for buyers and sellers to get together for a real estate transaction without a real estate agent. It advertised itself as a way to save money by not paying a commission. It was understandably very popular as every seller wants to make as much money as they can.

But Mr. Sambrotto had difficulty selling his luxury condo on that system.

After enough time had passed without a sale, he decided to engage a real estate agent. That agent charged him a 6% commission.

But that agent also sold that property for 7.5% *more* than the asking price Mr. Sambrotto had when selling the property privately. Not only did the agent succeed in selling where Mr. Sambrotto had failed, but he was also able to sell it for more money for Mr. Sambrotto even after his commission was deducted.

This story got headlines in many papers because it wasn't just a regular private seller who chose to switch from FSBO to a Realtor. This was the founder of a website that made himself very wealthy by charging for sale by owners. That the very owner of such a website had this experience is a pretty big slice of irony.

Which should you do? FSBO or Realtor?

Unfortunately, there is no one answer for everyone. It really depends on your situation. I know that feels like a cop-out of an answer, but it's the truth.

There is also nothing magical that a real estate agent does to succeed. It's all here in this book. It takes time, dedication, work, and experience to do it best – but nothing mysterious.

All that said, the above examples are excellent guides for which option is best for you.

If the criteria of when to consider selling yourself applies very well to you, and if the reasons to sell with a real estate agent do not apply to you, then it makes good sense to sell your property on your own. If you use the tips and strategies in this book, you are going to have a better chance of success compared to a home seller that doesn't.

If the criteria for considering to sell your property alone do not apply to you, or if the reasons to use a Realtor do, then you should use a Realtor. If you do, I'd recommend you choose one that has a marketing plan similar to this book.

Manufactured by Amazon.ca
Bolton, ON